I Need a Rich Home

Namdeo Bhagwandass

ISBN: 978-1-969564-22-2

CONTENTS

PREFACE

In a world bustling about in a cacophony of pursuits, where the glitter of gold and the almost hypnotic dance of affluence cloud our vision, it is easy to confuse shelter with home. A house, with its towering walls and ornate details, can boast of wealth, yet remain devoid of warmth. The chill of empty hallways may echo, revealing not the heartbeats of joyous gatherings, but the hollowness that comes from a life lived in pursuit of things rather than people. I invite you to untangle the threads woven deeply into our society—those threads of yearning and hope—that seek answers to what it truly means to possess a rich home. My purpose with this book is to carry you on a journey, as vivid as it is transformative, a journey that blossoms into a heartfelt anthem for souls yearning for a place that resonates with love, trust, and all the beauty that springs forth from genuine connection.

As you read the pages of "I NEED A RICH HOME," prepare yourself to walk alongside Mia, our vibrant protagonist, whose heart bears the weight of a world enamored with material wealth. Through her eyes, you will encounter the revolutionary realization that the true essence of a home cannot be quantified in bricks or elaborate decor—it lies nestled in the embrace of shared laughter, the comfort of understanding, and the nurture of authenticity. Those moments of quiet reflection, a gust of laughter shared with friends, or a fleeting snapshot of connection are what define a home, breathing life into its very foundation. Through Mia's journey, I hope you, too, will awaken to the incredible truth that richness is not always measured by what we have but often by who we are surrounded by, the unbreakable bonds we create, and the love we cultivate.

As Mia gallivants through landscapes vibrant with colour and texture, each chapter offers a different facet of this intricate jewel of a life, unearthing profound lessons that have lain dormant under the clutches of superficiality. From an elderly artisan who wields clay like a maestro or a wise monk who teaches her about inner wealth, the cast of characters opens their hearts, offering nuggets of wisdom that resonate with an ancient truth: that love is the greatest wealth we can possess. They remind us that trustworthiness, honesty, and the sacred act of connecting with one another are not merely lofty ideals to aspire towards but fundamental columns upon which balconies of joy can be built.

In every heartbeat of the narrative lies an exploration of themes that seek to harmonize the soul's yearning for richness. Togetherness emerges as a constant refrain, a reminder that in community and camaraderie, we find strength—the very energy that fuels the pursuit of something fulfilled and meaningful. The juxtaposition of scarcity in a material sense against an outpouring of generosity enriches not just relationships but infuses life with a vibrancy often missed in the routines of our busy, distraction-laden days. It is only when we learn to give of ourselves without holding back, engaging fully with those around us, that the concept of a "home" transforms from a mere residence into an abundant sanctuary, one enriched by shared experiences and mutual nurturing. As you travel through these pages, you will witness Mia, as she contemplates the fragility of family legacies, grappling with the complexities that can bind or liberate one's heart. In reclaiming her ancestral home—a treasure long thought lost—there unfolds a beautiful juxtaposition of the physical and the spiritual; a revelation that she isn't merely rediscovering a structure, but an archetype of love, a repository of lessons etched into the very walls, waiting patiently for her to awaken to the stories they breathe. It is here that the true climax of her journey awaits, the unravelling of a rich tapestry woven together, not only through her family's history but also intertwined with the lives she encounters.

This book is not merely a tale narrated for the sake of entertainment; it is a reflection designed for your heart. As the narratives entwine with dynamic experiences, I urge you to pause and reflect on your own life’s fabric. What does your home mean to you? What hidden treasures lie beneath the surface of your relationships? In the exploration of Mia’s journey, I hope you uncover facets of your essence, discovering the profound beauty waiting to be embraced.

So, dear reader, I invite you to settle in, take a deep breath, and perhaps let the walls that shield your heart down, even just a little. Open your spirit to the very possibility that a rich home does not consist solely of things you can see or touch, but rather of the love that envelops you like a warm evening breeze. The journey ahead promises to rekindle the flame of hope and the relentless pursuit of a life not shackled by mere existence, but blossoming in sincerity, authenticity, and joy. Together, let us uncover the clarity of home, where true richness unfolds beyond the tangible, into the profound, illuminating each precious fragment of life that connects us all.

1

THE CRUMBLING WALLS OF WEALTH

Mia stepped into the grand foyer of her home; a vast expanse filled with gleaming marble floors that reflected the light pouring in through crystal chandeliers. Each facet of the chandelier sparkled like the stars caught in a net of delicate glass, illuminating the opulence that surrounded her. She absently watched as the golden rays danced across the walls, crafted with intricate mouldings and adorned with lavish paintings that depicted scenes of historical elegance. Yet, amidst this splendour, an unsettling emptiness gnawed at her heart. The luxurious materials that painted her surroundings—silk drapes, ornate furniture, and exquisite decor—might have dazzled the eyes, but they left a chill in their wake, a coldness that settled deep within her soul. It became increasingly evident that something vital was amiss in this beautiful but hollow house.

As she wandered deeper into the vast expanse of her home, the echo of her steps reverberated through the emptiness, each sound a reminder of the distance that existed between her and the life she truly desired. The spaces that should have echoed with laughter and vibrant conversations were instead filled with silence, a dissonant chord playing between the lavishness of her surroundings and her yearning heart. Mia paused in front of a magnificent mirror framed in gold, her own reflection staring back at her—a reflection she hardly recognized. Dressed in fine silks that hugged her form perfectly, she appeared every bit the picture of success. Yet the vanity that accompanied her attire felt foreign on her skin, a gilded cage that adorned her rather than offered any semblance of authenticity or warmth.

The golden cage of her existence seemed exceptionally cruel as she traced her fingers over the surface of the polished wood of a nearby table, its smoothness in stark contrast to the jagged edges of her emotions. Memories flitted through her mind like ephemeral shadows—occasions where the air had been thick with camaraderie, where spontaneous laughter filled the space, where every corner exuded the scent of shared meals and stories woven together. Yet here she stood, cloaked in layers of luxury that created a barrier between her and the world outside, leaving her feeling as though she were on display, a living art piece devoid of connection. Each day blurred together in this grand setting, punctuated only by hollow parties and the sound of clinking glasses that didn't quite mask the absence of genuine interaction. She could almost hear her own thoughts echoing back to her against the lavishness of the walls, haunting her with their truth.

She thought of her childhood, when home was a cacophony of voices and smells, of warmth radiating from an open oven and giggles spilling from the porch as they played under the sun. Those are the moments she longed for, the moments when love consumed every corner of the house—love in the form of her mother's warm embrace, her siblings' laughter, and even the unguarded conversations with her father. Each one a thread in the fabric of her identity, binding her to moments that her current surroundings lacked. Instead, this affluent cage left her wondering whether it would be too much to ask for authenticity and connection amidst the shine and glamour. The exquisite façade began to warp into a surreal mirage, illuminating the truth she desperately tried to suppress.

On her journey through echoing hallways, she found herself in the lavishly appointed living room, staring at a grand piano that sat untouched, coated in a thin layer of dust. It was strikingly beautiful, yet it felt like nothing more than a prop in her life's play, a symbol of potential ignored. If she were being honest with herself, she couldn't recall the last time she had played—where had the joy gone? The notes that once spilled forth so easily now seemed trapped beneath the surface, like the vibrant hues of paint locked away within a pristine box. And what of the music she had loved so much? It had been replaced with the superficial melodies of parties and gatherings; each note a reminder of the void she had created between herself and the beauty of genuine expression.

Mia sank onto the plush upholstery of a sofa so elegantly designed that it became almost uncomfortable. She closed her eyes, wishing to escape the luxurious confines of her surroundings, conjuring images of a home where love was the air that was breathed and connections were forged through unspoken understanding. She craved the simplicity she had once known—the small joys of shared meals cooked together, an unhurried afternoon filled with conversation, and the unconditional love of friends and family. Instead, she found herself trapped within the gilded frame of her life, where every precious item had been curated but not nurtured, every beautiful artifice concealing the reality that she had become a stranger even to herself.

Suddenly, a sound broke into her reverie—the hushed rustle of the wind outside, whispering through the trees that bordered her estate. It beckoned her, inviting her to step outside this opulent prison and rediscover the world beyond. She yearned for the warmth of a summer breeze against her skin, the simple pleasure of grass beneath her bare feet, the laughter of children playing in the neighbourhood, and even the unscripted moments that came with genuine connections. The nature that thrived just beyond her home felt distant from her reality, as if enjoying such pleasures belonged only to those who lived in less adorned spaces, in places where life was more immediate and tangible.

In that instance, Mia felt a resolve brewing within her—an awakening that called for change. The desire to reclaim the essence of home burned brightly against the cold luxury that threatened to smother it. The realization loomed larger than her golden cage; the opulence surrounding her no longer gratified her. She resolved to step outside and face the world brimming with raw emotion, spontaneity, and human connection, even if it meant leaving behind the polished comfort she had always known. The thought invigorated her—a wild promise of freedom from the confines of her carefully curated existence. Mia felt the stirrings of hope, a signal that there lay a rich life waiting for her to embrace it that radiated far beyond the walls of her golden cage.

As she approached the grand entrance, certain phrases echoed back to her—'Life is too short; seek the meaning beyond material.' With each step towards the door, it dawned on her that wealth does not lie in the luxurious materials encasing her but in the relationships that flourish through shared experiences and unfiltered emotions. In this moment of clarity, Mia vowed that she would seek to forge her definition of a rich home—a place where laughter resonated off the walls, warmth overflowed in every corner, and love was the central pillar that anchored her heart and spirit.

As she contemplated her isolated existence, a sound broke through the stillness—laughter. A burst of joy, infectious and genuine, floated through an open window, drawing her outside like a moth to a flame. The world beyond her walls seemed to bloom vibrantly in contrast to the sterile beauty inside. Curiosity piqued, Mia stepped through the sliding glass door leading to the garden, where she discovered a group of children energetically playing, their laughter a melody of pure delight that sliced through her quiet despair. Their innocent joy tugged at her heartstrings, resonating with a yearning she hadn't realized was so deeply buried. One child in particular, a little girl with curly hair and bright eyes, danced freely beneath the sun, her spirit unbounded by the confines of privilege or appearance, illuminated by an inner light that spoke of hope and possibility. Mia couldn't help but smile, a genuine shift in her heart sparking to life at the sight of such unabashed happiness.

The children's laughter wove a tapestry of sound, but it was the little girl's exuberance that anchored Mia's attention—she twirled and leaped with a zest for life that felt infectious, and for the first time, Mia felt her heart flutter with something she had long thought dormant: a desire for connection. As the girl caught sight of her, she ran over, her face beaming with innocent enthusiasm. "Would you like to play with us?" she asked, her voice ringing like a sweet bell, filled with expectation. Mia hesitated, a wall of self-doubt and hesitation rising within her. She felt a pull, a yearning to join this world of raw, unrefined joy, yet the weight of societal expectations, as a twenty-two year old, and the invisible chains of her luxurious life held her back. But something deep inside stirred fervently, whispering that there was life beyond these walls—a life that thrived on shared laughter, playful connection, and the warmth of community.

Just then, as if sensing her conflict, the girl reached out her tiny hand, extending a bridge between Mia's clammy introspection and the vibrant world that lay just beyond her mansion, a world defined not by riches but by relationships. In that moment, all her doubts surrendered to an irresistible pull to break free from the constraints of her self-imposed solitude. Mia grasped the girl's hand, her fingers wrapping around the small palm that felt vibrant and alive with possibility. With each step she took towards the group, she felt the warmth of hope coursing through her veins, a sensation that began to melt away the chill of her existence. The children welcomed her with open arms, an unspoken invitation into their world where joy was a language they all spoke fluently, unshackled by the societal casing that often encloses adults in silence.

Playing tag with the children, Mia felt the years of isolation lift as laughter intertwined with the fragrant breeze, filling her lungs with a sense of vitality she had almost forgotten existed. Each rotation of her body, each chase across the sun-kissed grass, reawakened something dormant within her. As she darted alongside the children their laughter, a euphoric chorus that drowned out the whispers of her insecurities, the barriers she had built around herself began to crumble. In this ephemeral sanctuary, her soul danced freely, unburdened by the expectations that had once defined her. She felt light, liberated as if the childish thrill of running and laughing was igniting forgotten embers of contentment within her heart.

Time ceased to exist as Mia found herself relishing the richness of this shared experience. She witnessed how the children relied on one another; their innocent trust forged bonds that defied their worldly circumstances. They didn't care about the trappings of wealth, nor did they seek validation through material possessions; instead, their lives were vivid with possibilities spun from laughter, shared dreams, and unconditional love. This contrast—the sharp awareness of her own loneliness against the backdrop of communal care—became a catalyst for a heartfelt realization: wealth was not found in refined silks or ornate chandeliers, but in the simplicity of connection, in the fundamental human experience of togetherness.

With dusk approaching, the sun dipped low, setting the sky ablaze with hues of gold and crimson, as if nature itself were celebrating the transformation that had occurred within Mia. She pulled the children close, planting herself firmly in their infectious joy, filled with the knowledge that she was no longer adrift. In their innocent embrace, she discovered the stirring of dreams not weighed down by expectations but buoyed by the pure delight of simply being. Moments spent in a crafted and manicured yard paled in comparison with her newfound companions; it was the laughter that reverberated through the air, a melody underscoring the importance of presence, of existing fully in the moment.

Returning to the opulence of her home, the grandeur felt less intimidating; rather, it became a blank canvas waiting for her to infuse it with the life her heart so desperately craved. In the flickering light of hope ignited by her encounter, Mia began to envision the transformation her house could undergo. Instead of cold, lonely walls, Mia could fill them with warmth and connection, reviving lost dreams as she set forth to reclaim her identity. As she shut the door behind her, she carried with her not only the laughter of children but the clarity of purpose that reverberated in her soul. In that moment, she understood that a rich home was not dictated by currency or material possessions, but by the passionate embrace of love, warmth, and hope, all waiting patiently to be cultivated and cherished.

2

THE QUEST FOR AUTHENTICITY

The next day Mia meandered through the vibrant streets, the laughter and sounds of joy danced in the air like notes from an enchanting melody, wrapping around her and beckoning her to join in the celebration of life that surrounded her. The colours were alive—painted walls adorned with the art of those who found beauty in their surroundings, flowers symphonizing in hues of yellow and purple, and laughter spilling onto the cobblestones from little children who chased each other while their parents watched on with beaming smiles. It was in this lively atmosphere that Mia felt her heart wither lovingly, yearning to understand how such warmth could exist when she herself felt like a haunted fragment of someone who once thrived in the embrace of companionship. She wandered deeper into the labyrinth of creativity and companionship, her senses alight with possibility, until she stumbled upon a small, unassuming workshop nestled between two jubilant storefronts. The sign hanging above the entrance read: "The Artisan's Touch."

Intrigued, Mia pushed the door open and entered, the soft chime of a bell announcing her presence. The fragrant aroma of wet clay, mingling with the faint scent of incense, enveloped her like a warm hug. The scene inside was a delightful contrast to the bustling streets just beyond the threshold; it felt intimate, as though the walls themselves whispered secrets of craftsmanship and heritage. In the corner sat the potter—a humble figure with hands that seemed to dance rhythmically over a spinning wheel, creating art as he shaped the raw clay into exquisite vessels. His hair was peppered with gray, a testament to years spent nurturing not just the clay, but the connections that filled his heart with purpose. Mia stood transfixed, the creation process hypnotizing as the potter moulded the formless earth into something magnificent.

"Come in, dear one," he smiled, glancing up from his work, his eyes twinkling with the wisdom of experience. "You look like someone in search of something." His voice was soothing, like a calming breeze caressing weary travelers. Mia stepped closer, the warmth radiating from the pottery, absorbing her soul, beckoning to the yearning she felt simmering within her.

"I am, indeed," she confessed, glancing around at the finished pieces displayed around the workshop—a collective of vases, bowls, and sculptures, each a testament to the love and care infused into them. Each item whispered its story of humble beginnings, conceived in the clay of the earth and brought to life through the gentle persistence of a master hand. "I've travelled looking for… what a home truly means, but I am lost amidst the noise of it all."

The potter leaned back, placing his hands in his lap, the raw clay cool between his fingers. He observed Mia with a tenderness reserved for those who came seeking understanding. "A home is not merely the walls that surround you, my dear. It is the warmth you feel when love is present; it's trust nurtured through shared moments. Each pot here began as a formless blob of clay, just like you may feel—without direction or purpose. As artists, we learn to see the potential within that simplicity. Come, feel it."

With hesitant excitement, Mia stepped forward, and the potter guided her hands to the cool, wet clay. The sensation was electric; the clay felt alive beneath her touch, moist and pliable, reflecting the very essence of possibility. "Your hands, my dear, can be an extension of your heart."

"Once, many years ago," the potter began, as if weaving a tapestry with his voice that mingled with the rhythm of the spinning wheel. "I was in your shoes—searching and questioning what it meant to belong, yearning for recognition in a world that often values only the material. I found clarity through my craft. Each piece I've created tells a story, and every imperfection contains a lesson. You see, while the world debates the worth of a thing based on money, it is the heart and soul of the maker embedded in the creation that truly holds value."

His words resonated with Mia deeply. She envisioned herself in a cozy home, a place infused not with the coldness of money but with the warmth of love and kindness. She realized that it was resilience and trust in the process of creation—of both art and relationships—that founded a rich home. The intricacies of pulling together a close-knit family relied not on extravagant dinners or lavish gifts but manifested in small, simple moments of love shared around the kitchen table or the laughter shared over a cup of tea as stories unfolded through eager exchanges. Inspired by the Artisan's gentle wisdom, Mia felt lighter, as if the burdens she had been carrying evaporated like morning mist under the sun. The Artisan's Touch was alive, a space filled with magic where time ceased to matter, and resilience flourished like wildflowers in a sun-drenched meadow. Deep within her, a recognition blossomed; this small workshop, lit by shafts of sunlight intermingling with dust, had become a sacred space she never knew she needed, a home carved from love and connection. It was here, in the embrace of clay and creativity, that Mia would plant the seeds of hope, and with the wisdom from the potter, she would cultivate a life where her heart could dwell without the overshadowing weight of material triumphs. The rich home she sought was one where laughter harmonized with trust, and warmth enveloped every gathering—a place where her spirit could unwind and flourish, nurtured by the love she intended to sew among her community.

Mia's encounter made her determined now more than ever to reclaim her legacy, her ancestral roots, and forge ahead with an open heart, ready to create a sanctuary alive with the laughter, love, and warmth of those who would gather around her. She could envision a space vibrating with life, a home filled not with things but with connections—warm embraces, heartfelt conversations, and shared stories that would fill the air like the soft strains of a beloved melody, marking the true beginning of her journey toward finding a rich home already paid for with love and connection, one that was waiting for her to uncover its depths.

Her heart filled with an insatiable hunger for more of these relationships—each connection deepening her sense of home beyond brick and mortar. In every person she met, she discovered reflections of herself; their joys, struggles, and resilience spoke to the universal search for acceptance and love. With each shared laugh and moment of silence, she found herself more emboldened, layering her life experiences with the richness of others' stories. It was as if this newly formed mosaic of relationships breathed life into her once-isolated spirit, reminding her that true wealth is found not in solitude, but in the intricate dance of humanity united by shared hopes and dreams.

As days turned into weeks, Mia found solace in the very essence of connection. She began to spend her evenings at the town square, where friends gathered to share tales beneath the captivating glow of twinkling stars. The presence of community enveloped her like a warm embrace, coaxing her from her shell and reminding her of a time when laughter echoed through her home, once filled with the love of family. Discussions often meandered into philosophies of life, dreams interwoven with notions of peace and contentment. The diverse perspectives illuminated paths she had yet to traverse, urging her to explore not just the world around her but the intricate landscapes within her own heart.

One evening, as the sun dipped low, painting the sky in hues of orange and pink, Mia found herself sharing her own story with newfound friends. Words flowed as she poured her heart out, revealing her struggles and the quest—a seeker yearning for a home forged from love and trust. Suddenly, the vulnerable sharing of her truth felt like a powerful act of connection in itself; each word resonated in the hearts of others, drawing them closer as they shared their stories with her. Her narrative echoed the sentiments of many who had sought solace and kinship in an increasingly fractured world. This bond forged through honesty and authenticity felt ineffable, a testament to the strength found in vulnerability.

With each passing day, Mia learned that finding connection was not just about interaction; it was an experience steeped in reciprocity that required her heart to be open, willing to receive and give in equal measure. She found herself blossoming, nourished by the rich soil of community. The weight of her loneliness began to lift, replaced by the comforting realization that she was indelibly woven into a larger tapestry—each thread representing a life, a journey, and a connection that enriched not only her own existence but those of others around her. The laughter now echoed in her chest, filling the void that had once consumed her as memories amassed, promising a future laced with joy, sincerity, and deep trust.

The vibrant streets of her new reality mirrored the abundance she craved, and Mia felt fortunate to have stumbled into this world that embraced her past struggles and transformed them into lessons of hope and resilience. Each laugh, each tear, every shared meal became part of a newfound home where the bonds of love flourished. She understood now that while physical homes may come and go, it is the connections nurtured within us that build the real sanctuary—the rich home she had yearned for all along. The realization enveloped her like a warm quilt, reminding her that no matter how tumultuous her journey had been, she was never truly alone. A web of connection enveloped her, affirming that she was an essential part of the fabric of countless lives intertwined, forever changed by shared stories and warm hearts.

3

BREAKING DOWN WALLS

As the sun began its slow descent behind the mountains, casting long shadows that danced playfully across the cobblestone streets of the quaint village, Mia still carried the weight of her realizations heavy on her heart. She had spent days feeling lost, the burden of her empty pursuits weighing down her spirit. Despite the colorful life surrounding her—the laughter of children playing in the distance, the scent of freshly baked bread wafting through the air—her soul felt like an echoing chamber, void of the warmth she so craved. It was on this particular evening, however, that she found herself sitting on a weathered bench in the village square, the warmth of the wood resonating through her, an old comfort like an embrace from a long-lost friend.

Here, she was joined by Oliver, a gentle soul she had met a few days prior. With unruly curls framing his open and kind face, he had an authenticity about him that drew her in. Oliver was unlike the other villagers she had encountered; he wore his heart as openly as he wore his passion for art. His laughter rang clear like a bell, cascading through the air, healing something within her that she hadn't even realized had been broken. It was an unspoken understanding that lingered between them, a connection that felt as effortless as the breeze that swayed the leaves overhead. Encouraged by the moment, Mia took a deep breath, the kind that unraveled her tightly knotted soul, and turned towards him.

"Can I tell you something?" she hesitated, feeling her vulnerability prick at her skin. Her voice trembled slightly as she caught his gaze, the warmth in those deep brown eyes urging her to continue.

With a slight nod, Oliver offered her a measure of reassurance that seemed to dissipate the walls she had meticulously built, made of pride and fear. "I've spent so long searching for happiness in places that seem so hollow now. I thought if I amassed the right things, surrounded myself with beautiful things, I would find fulfilment. But I feel so… so lost," she whispered, shame flickering in her chest. The admission hung in the air, thick and heavy, like the humidity that enveloped the summer evening, and she felt her heart race, scared of being exposed in such an intimate way.

Oliver shifted closer, his eyes reflecting empathy. "You're not alone in feeling that way. I've walked that path too. But real wealth comes from believing in ourselves and in those around us, in the bonds we make rather than the things we have." There was something about his authenticity, his uncomplicated way of viewing life, that had a sobering effect on her chaotic thoughts. As the silence stretched between them, Mia couldn't help but notice the magnificence of the evening sky, hues of purple and gold swirling together in an ethereal symphony, mirroring her emotional turmoil yet offering glimpses of possibility.

"Maybe it's time I learned to trust again," she murmured, more to herself than to Oliver. Her mind wandered back to her childhood, memories of laughter and play echoing through the halls of her family home. Yet, those memories had become distorted over the years, eclipsed by the shadows of resentment and disconnection that had seeped into her family relationships. Mia realized that trust was the very foundation upon which not just relationships—but homes—are built. The realization was overwhelming as she began to understand that she had been so cautious, so rigid in safeguarding her heart that she had neglected the beauty of friendship and connection right before her.

"What if," she continued, emboldened by Oliver's gentle presence, "I tried to break down the walls I've built? I can't keep hiding behind them." Her voice quivered with the enormity of what she was suggesting. In an age where vulnerability was often mistaken for weakness, she contemplated the beauty and strength in exposing her true self to others. Oliver smiled, faint but radiant, his sincerity reflecting what she had yearned for—a bond created through authenticity.

"I believe that's the first step toward building something beautiful; transforming the space we occupy from mere existence into a sanctuary," he replied, an edge of warmth lacing his words. Mia's heart fluttered at the thought. It was in that moment of shared understanding that she felt the first glimmers of hope. She wondered if emotions did indeed have the power to break down walls, to renew her outlook on relationships. It would take courage, the kind she was finally beginning to muster, to allow herself to be vulnerable.

The sun dipped lower, blurring the boundaries of day and night, and in that transitional space, Mia sensed the enormity of her own potential. A rush of excitement coursed through her as she realized that with trust comes openness. It meant allowing others in, sharing laughter and tears, and allowing joy to filter through the mess of life. It meant creating a community that encompassed genuine connections forged not in transaction but in sincere exchange.

As their conversation deepened, and the evening stretched luxuriously around them, she shared stories from her life—the bittersweet tales of laughter and loss. Each word was a brick, each laughter an invitation to forge a space where honesty and openness reigned supreme. For every secret she unveiled, a slice of her heart slowly peeled back, unveiling raw and aching truths: her childhood fears, her longing for acceptance, the place she had always called home—the good, the bad, and everything in between. Oliver listened intently, never interrupting, allowing Mia's experiences to hang in the air as an invitation and a sign of solidarity.

Mia felt lighter with every word, as if the invisible chains that bound her heart began to loosen their claim. Each story became a catalyst for her understanding of what it meant to trust and be trusted. She realized that trust was not merely an abstract idea but rather a tangible force that knit people together, supporting them in moments of triumph and holding them closely during times of adversity. It was, perhaps, in the sharing, in the bridge built between hearts, that true wealth resided.

As darkness enveloped the village, painted with twinkling stars and the gentle whisper of the wind, Mia's heart swelled with gratitude. She sensed that this newfound friendship with Oliver was the seed from which her journey towards rebuilding her understanding of home would bloom. She envisioned herself, arms wide open, surrounded by a loving community where vulnerability was embraced as strength. As if reading her thoughts, Oliver remarked, "Home isn't just a structure; it's the people we choose to share our lives with. You honour those bonds by nurturing them, being present in their moments, and allowing them to show up for you."

A smile broke through the strands of her introspection, and laughter bubbled within her, like the dawn after a long night. "You're right. I need to stop clinging to what I thought I lost. I must embrace the possibility of rebuilding—brick by brick, heart by heart." This conversational exchange transformed into a promise to Mia, a vow to redesign her outlook, weave the threads of connection, and let the joy of shared existence wash over her. As she looked into Oliver's encouraging eyes, she understood that these walls she long held had not only confined her but also shielded her from the warmth of affection she yearned for.

In that moment, beneath the vast expanse of the evening sky, Mia felt as if she were unfurling, the layers of her heart peeling away like petals of a blooming flower, ready to soak up the sunlight of love and trust. She was learning that breaking down the walls wasn't merely about exposing herself; it was also about inviting others to walk with her, fostering relationships that would become the essence of a rich home. Their voices faded softly into the night, intermingling with the chorus of crickets, a celebration of newfound trust growing stronger, louder, and more vibrant—a true home unfolding within her heart.

4

TRUST IN ACTION

Mia stood at the threshold of realization, the afternoon light curling through the tall grasses of the meadow, casting a golden hue that seemed to capture the very essence of her emotions. It was in this serene moment of vulnerability that she felt the whisper of connection, a shadow of an embrace she had been yearning for her entire life. She had spent so much time navigating the tumultuous waters of superficial relationships, where trust was a bargaining chip, easily given but rarely reciprocity in the exchange. Yet, here in this expansive space, surrounded by wild blooms and the gentle hum of nature, she began to understand that trust was not merely a line drawn in the sand, but an ever-evolving tapestry woven together from the threads of honesty, shared experiences, and vulnerability.

The surface of what she perceived as her own fears slowly cracked under the weight of warmth emanating from the earnest eyes of those she had met throughout her journey. As she stood in the meadow, her heart raced with a mixture of trepidation and hope. This realization didn't come easily; there was something transformative about admitting her own insecurities. She had been wrestling with the stigma of her solitary existence, often feeling as if she were the lone star in a vast, indifferent universe. Yet, the resonance of community echoed through her, urging her to embrace this moment of vulnerability. She recalled her encounter with the Elder, an iconic figure whose presence always seemed to radiate wisdom. He had said to her at their last meeting beneath the grand oak tree, "Mia, trust is forged in fire, often borne out of uncertainty. It is an invitation to be seen, to expose your fears and share your dreams." His words danced in her mind, igniting embers of courage, and Mia felt compelled to reflect on where she had been placing her trust up until now. It dawned on her that she had sought trust in grand gestures and extravagant promises instead of the quiet authenticity found in everyday moments, steeped in genuine connection.

As the sun dipped lower in the sky, she chose to cross that threshold into vulnerability. She invited a small group of newfound friends—a quirky artist, a spirited storyteller, and a nurturing gardener—to join her in the meadow for a simple picnic. It was a gesture that felt monumental to her, exposing bits of her heart she had long hidden. As they gathered on the soft grass, laughter mingled with the soft breeze, and the ease of their shared presence began to dissolve the remnants of her anxiety. Mia felt the threads of trust weaving together as she opened up about her fears, her dreams, and the longing for a place that felt like home, not in terms of bricks and walls, but as an emotional sanctuary. Each friend responded with stories of their own, peeling back layers to reveal their own vulnerabilities. It was not merely a collection of words being exchanged; it was a dance of souls, a celebration of the shared human experience that mirrored her own truth.

In those moments, she sensed the weight of connection anchoring deeper, solidifying the foundation that would support their relationships. Trust thrived in the authenticity of their exchanges. When they spoke, it was not just with their mouths; they spoke with their hearts and souls, drawing on experiences that echoed the vibrancy of their individual paths. The artist shared a story filled with struggle and resilience, revealing how the act of creation had salvaged fragments of his spirit over the years, while the storyteller spun tales that felt simultaneously ancient and deeply personal, invoking a sense of belonging that transcended time. The gardener, with her soothing presence, shared how her nurturing of plants mirrored her nurturing of relationships—both requiring patience, openness, and, above all, a willingness to trust in the cycle of life. It was a reminder that the act of letting go and allowing others in was essential to cultivating not only their blooms but the relationships that enabled them to flourish.

Mia realized how profoundly their shared vulnerability had deepened their connection. No longer were they merely acquaintances bound by circumstance; they had transformed into a tapestry of intertwining lives, each thread rich with trust and sincerity. The shared fears, ambitions, and joys formed a bond that resonated like a symphony, where every voice contributed to a greater harmony. With every laugh and tear shed that evening, they constructed an invisible lattice of support, one that energized their hearts—an unshakeable foundation upon which each could stand and flourish.

It was then that Mia understood trust not as a singular act but as an ongoing exchange: an intricate dance that invites vulnerability and breathes life into relationships. This collective experience became the soil in which trust could grow, nurtured by the roots of empathy and understanding, allowing it to blossom into something far more profound than she had ever imagined. As darkness draped the meadow like a soothing quilt, punctuated by the twinkling of stars, Mia's heart brimmed with a luminous warmth, a flame sparked by the trust she had begun to cultivate with those around her. She was forging connections that transcended mere social constructs, establishing bonds that echoed through the chambers of her spirit.

With this renewed understanding, Mia took the opportunity to establish a deeper connection with each person present. She began asking questions that would invite them to share not just their stories but their dreams, their aspirations, and even their fears. Each inquiry revealed layers she hadn't anticipated, exposing paths that added richer colours to the fabric of their collective narrative. It was fascinating for Mia to witness how each individual carried their unique burdens and joys, yet here they were, united in this small space, aiming to nurture bonds that felt grounded in mutual understanding. She relished the way trust blossomed in each shared story, how stories unspooled like threads, revealing new possibilities that connected them in ways even the vastness of the world couldn't sever. Each revelation became a tiny seed, implanted in the soil of their relationships, germinating trust as they celebrated their shared triumphs and tribulations.

The very act of participating in each other's lives transformed Mia's earlier feelings of isolation into a vibrant sense of belonging. As they shared their hopes and fears, she sensed the shift not just in herself but also in her friends. They leaned closer, captivated not just by the tales being told but by the realization that trust begets trust. The tapestry of their trust began expanding, weaving together diverse threads of backgrounds and experiences, united under the shared banner of humanity itself. Each story they exchanged was not just an isolated instance but became part of a grand narrative, one that shaped their understanding of home as a collection of the heartfelt stories and bonds they built over these moments together.

Underneath the vastness of the starlit sky, this collective sharing was a testimony to the power of vulnerability—a reminder that foolishness might not reside in shared fears but in the silence, we sometimes choose to maintain in the presence of others. As they laid together on the soft grass, gazing at the cosmos above, Mia felt a sense of peace, her heart vibrating with the awareness that she was no longer alone in her yearnings. In the melodies of laughter and shared dreams, she heard the rhythm of trust — a song that echoed in the corners of her soul, enriching her sense of what it truly meant to have a home.

She felt the sacred art of trust in action—the very essence of what would allow her to reclaim the ancestral home she had once believed to be a mere structure of bricks and mortar. Instead, it was redefined now, rooted in the myriad connections her heart was beginning to forge. Little did she know that this night would mark the beginning of a new chapter in her journey, showcasing the intangible wealth that arises not merely from the bonds we craft but the beauty inherent in the vulnerability we dare to embrace amidst the threads of human connection. And in that meadow, surrounded by blossoming friendships, Mia took the first steps in understanding that true richness lay not in the architecture of a house but in the joyful symphony of trust as it unravels into the tapestry of home.

5

EMBRACING HONESTY

Mia stood before the mirror, the morning sunlight filtering through the translucent curtains and casting dancing shadows across her reflection. The woman who gazed back at her was a stranger in some ways, yet familiar in others. Her heart raced, a symphony of emotions stirring within her as she contemplated the journey that had led her to this moment of reckoning. This was not just any reflection; it was a gateway to her inner self, a portal to her myriad truths. Her once-lustrous hair, now tinged with the fatigue of endless searching, framed her face like a halo that had lost its luminescence. It struck her then, that the perception of oneself is often clouded by external portrayals, the weight of societal expectations, and the haunting echoes of inadequacy that had followed her like shadows for far too long. Today, however, as she stood silently before the mirror, she resolved to peel back the layers and confront the haunting truths she had long evaded.

The echoes of her encounters with others reverberated within her mind—the wise Elder whose gentle words about authenticity lingered like a sweet perfume in the air, the serene Monk who had introduced her to the depth of her own spirit, and the Artisan with hands that mold clay into dreams. Each had gifted her lessons that cut deep into her understanding of what connection truly meant. It was with each interaction that Mia began to see the gaping cracks in the façade she'd maintained, the lies woven into the very fabric of her existence. It dawned on her that truthfulness was not merely a weapon to wield against the world but a gift to share—a foundation upon which meaningful connections could flourish. For too long, she had allowed the isolation of her guardedness to dictate her relationships, hiding behind walls constructed from fear and misconceptions. She thought of the carefully curated stories she shared, the partial truths that danced around her authentic self, and realized how these barriers had only served to keep others at bay.

As she scrutinized her reflection, Mia recognized the fierce hues of yearning in her deep-set eyes—the desire to be free from the entrapments of pretence. Each wrinkle of worry etched across her forehead; each line that spoke of sleepless nights and unanswered questions formed a roadmap of her experiences. Her face, though marked by uncertainty, mirrored a woman who was learning to embrace vulnerability. Stepping forward, she touched her fingertips to the cool surface of the glass, feeling an inexplicable connection to the woman she was discovering beneath the uncertainties of a materialistic world. The reflection shifted, morphing into a tapestry of all the loves she had known, the friendships she had sought, and the cracks she had become skilled at avoiding. She thought of Emelia, her childhood friend, whose laughter had once filled the corners of her heart—a laugh that felt muted in the presence of unexpressed deeper feelings. Mia had kept her conversations light and airy, fearing that opening up too much might unravel the threads of their friendship. Yet now, she longed for connection that traversed the superficial, yearning for the profound bond woven from understanding, empathy, and honesty.

With a sudden steadiness filling her spirit, Mia looked deeper, past the surface, examining the gossamer threads of love and fear that intertwined in her consciousness. She remembered the late-night confessions shared with her brother, so often smothered by unsaid words—lessons about honesty she had failed to heed. There was a raw yearning within her to mend that bridge, understanding now that it was through facing the truths of their experiences that a more profound, unshakeable bond could arise. No longer could she allow shame and fear to dictate the landscape of her connections; she was ready to rewrite those narratives, to shape them with gratitude and grace. The thought traversed through her mind like an unrelenting wave. This moment of solitude in front of the mirror was not merely an introspective exercise; it was a catalyst for transformation.

Mia took a breath, allowing the freshness of the morning air to seep into her being and instil her with courage. The idea of exposing her soul felt as close to terrifying as it was exhilarating—like standing on the edge of an unfathomable abyss, ready to leap into the unknown. She remembered the Elder's teachings about trustworthiness—the essence of forging connections that transcended the material world. Trust was a delicate thread spun from time, experiences, and shared truths, but it was also an act of faith, an openness to vulnerability that Mia had thus far been reluctant to embrace. It was time to drop the masks that had shrouded her essence for far too long.

Amidst the deep reflection, she envisioned her late grandmother's home, filled with the scent of baking bread, where laughter weaved through the air like a melody. It was a sanctuary of honesty and warmth, rich in the simplest of luxuries—a place where stories were exchanged like currency, and love was the wealth that dominated the atmosphere. It struck her how richness was not crafted through intricate tapestries of material possession but was manifested in moments of shared laughter, the acceptance of flaws, and the freedom found in being completely oneself. The invisible bonds forged during those innocent moments had sculpted her heart, and Mia realized she wanted to replicate that essence in her journey forward. She wanted her home to be a sanctuary brimming with love, a vibrant tapestry woven from genuine relationships enriching her life more than any tangible possession ever could.

With newfound clarity coursing through her heart, Mia stepped back from the mirror, the sadness and yearning bubbling to the surface like a wellspring bursting forth. She understood now that she could no longer hide from her honesty or seek worthiness through comparison. Instead, it was time to embrace her past, flawed yet irreplaceable. Each experience had contributed to her understanding of home—the warmth, the chaos, the laughter over evening meals shared in twilight—and had now nudged her toward this pivotal moment of awakening. It wasn't merely about reclaiming a family home thought lost; it was about rediscovering the richness nestled within, the essence that followed even through the darkest nights.

This realization swept through her like a warm embrace, washing over the doubts that had long clung like chains to her spirit. Mia felt a lightness within, knowing she was no longer alone in her quest. The struggles of her past were not isolated experiences meant to haunt her, but rather threads in the tapestry of her life inviting her to sew a new narrative, one that embraced truthfulness as its guiding principle. The journey ahead was uncertain, but it was filled with promise—a sacred path towards vulnerability and authenticity that would enlighten her spirit and reawaken her sense of belonging.

As she disengaged completely from her reflection, not seeking closure but rather an open door to her future, Mia felt the rush of hope blossoming in her heart. It was time to seek connections that flourished in the light of truth, kindled by shared laughter, kindness, and trust. Clenching her fists, she felt the weight of the fleeting moment settle softly upon her shoulders; it was as if the universe had been waiting patiently for this very embrace of self-discovery. The world outside awaited her unveiling; it was an enthusiastic beckoning towards a life of sincerity, where the richness of her soul would shine through like sunlight breaking through the clouds. Deep within, she recognized that she was on the precipice of greatness—not through the acquisition of wealth or possessions, but through the integrity of her heart and the sincerity of her connections. As she propelled herself into her new journey, she no longer sought a rich home in terms of possessions but instead resolved to craft one where love reigned supreme, generously shared among those graced to enter her life.

6

THE HONEST EXCHANGE

The sun dipped low on the horizon, casting a golden hue across the landscape as Mia sat on a weathered bench in the town square, her heart full yet restless, longing for something that had evaded her grasp for far too long. It was a small square, bustling with life; children chased after one another, their laughter harmonizing with the gentle whispers of the wind. But amidst the joyful chaos, Mia felt a heaviness in her chest, an unsettled yearning for clarity. Around her, the vibrant market stalls overflowed with handcrafted wares, each one telling a story, but she ached for a different kind of exchange—a raw, sincere connection that transcended material bounds. As she sat there, the echoes of her realizations reverberated within her, nudging her to seek out the genuine in a world so often cloaked in facades.

It wasn't long before she noticed an elderly woman approaching, stooped yet unyielding, with eyes that sparkled with the wisdom of countless seasons. The woman carried with her an air of calm, and as she settled on the bench beside Mia, there was an unspoken understanding that passed between them. Mia felt an instinctive urge to speak, to peel back the layers of her heart and reveal her deepest struggles and hopes. As they exchanged polite pleasantries, the woman's gaze prompted Mia to dig deeper, urging her to share what lay beneath her surface.

"There's a restlessness within me," Mia confessed, her voice barely above a whisper, as if the very act of speaking her truth unleashed something profound. "I feel lost in this pursuit of a rich home, one that seems so unattainable despite the beauty that surrounds me. I thought wealth could be found in shiny things, but now I realize it's something far more substantial, something that requires uncovering." The woman listened intently, her face calm and knowing, a gentle smile unfurling as she nodded, inviting Mia to continue her unburdening.

"Everywhere I go, people chase after things that glitter, but what about the glow that lies within? What about love, trust, and honesty? I've met people who seem to embody these qualities, but as soon as they talk of their achievements, their homes filled with expensive possessions, I find myself retreating into loneliness. How could anyone prize genuine connection above status?" The words spilled out, raw and unfiltered, and as they did, a steady stream of emotions welled up within her, each one tethered to the heartbeat of her longing.

The woman turned her gaze toward the distant horizon, allowing the moment to linger before she spoke. "Ah, my dear, you've touched upon the very essence of what it means to be human—our experiences, our relationships, our honesty in conversation. Each of those things weave together the fabric of a home far more gratifying than any grand estate can provide. Honesty can be like an open window, allowing light and air to flow in, but it also requires vulnerability, a willingness to expose the soft, frail parts of us the world may overlook." There was a shimmer of understanding in her voice that captured Mia's attention. This was not just a conversation; it was a warm embrace of shared truths, each word binding them steadily to one another.

Encouraged by the woman's sincerity, Mia reflected on a time when she had stumbled upon the beauty of honesty in an unexpected encounter. "Not long ago, I spent time with an artisan, someone whose hands brought life to the mundane. He showed me how he shaped clay, how each piece he created became an expression of joy and heartache woven together. I remember him telling me that to truly create, one must pour their soul into the work—no mask, no pretense. I thought of that as I tried to piece together the fragments of my own life, where my heart and my facade seem so disjointed, battling within. How do we get to a point where we can be authentic in our exchanges?"

The elderly woman smiled, her eyes sparkling with shared understanding. "That's the crux of it, isn't it? To expose oneself requires an extraordinary courage, a leap of faith that many fear to take. In a world vying for attention, true intimacy comes when we bare our souls not in the hope of recognition, but rather out of a genuine desire to share. That's the beauty of honesty—the moment we allow ourselves to be vulnerable, others often respond in kind. Think back to the artisan. Did he not invite you into his world by revealing his truest self?"

With an awakening heart, Mia felt the warmth of that realization spread through her. The memories flooded back—how the artisan spoke about his creations, each vessel holding not just clay but fragments of his existence, his dreams, and his struggles. It was then that she understood that in those moments, they built a bridge of connection, authentically embracing each other as they shared laughter and heartache alike. "Yes, yes! He did open himself up to me, and it felt like I was gazing into the soul of the clay he shaped, each piece imbued with his story. Perhaps if I allow myself to cultivate such exchanges, I could carve out a richness in my life that no amount of money could buy."

The woman nodded knowingly as Mia's expression deepened in realization. "Imagine crafting a sanctuary not just from bricks and mortar, but from the very emotions you share. When we exchange our truths with another, we grant them the keys to the home we build within ourselves, equipped with all the comforts of compassion and truth. You see, the honest exchange creates a tapestry of experiences where each thread strengthens the bonds of trust and love."

Mia felt as if the heavens had opened before her; the weight she had carried dissipated like morning fog. She could envision her life not merely as a path towards elusive goals, but rather as a journey filled with meaningful encounters, where each exchange brought forth opportunities for connection—a rich home, indeed, built upon the sanctity of truthfulness. Strengthened by this new perspective, she spoke, her voice steady, "I wish to be like that artisan, to bring beauty out of vulnerability, to express every ounce of my being in those exchanges. I want to be brave enough to let others glimpse the world within me."

The woman's eyes sparkled again, as if Mia's words had reignited the fire within her heart. "That, my dear, is the first step towards the life you seek. To be rich in heart, to surround yourself with genuine connections forged through honesty; that is to weave love into your very being, creating a sanctuary that resonates with the warmth of your spirit. We are not defined by what we possess, but rather how we choose to share our stories with others. Trust your journey and embrace the unearthed treasures you find along the way. The more open and vulnerable you are, the more genuine connections will bloom around you."

The honest exchange had unshackled her from unfulfilling pursuits, guiding her toward a life steeped in authenticity. She turned towards the elderly woman, palpable gratitude filling her heart, overwhelmed by the gift of shared wisdom, a forever testament to the power of connection. The shadows began to stretch long and deep around them, yet inside her, a soft light shone brightly, a beacon guiding her forward. With every honest conversation she would seek, she knew she would discover not just the richness of a home, but the beauty of the human spirit intertwined in the tapestry of life. As they shared another smile, Mia could feel the universe conspiring to bring her closer to the home she had been seeking, not in any manifested wealth but in the priceless treasure of connection and a warm embrace of love that awaited her just beyond the horizon.

7

BUILDING ON TRUTH

Mia stood on the edge of a sun-drenched meadow, the golden rays caressing her skin as a gentle breeze danced playfully with the tall grass. The open space before her seemed as vast as the potential she felt bubbling within. It was here, in this serene setting, that she began to unravel the essence of truth in her interactions. Her journey had already guided her to wonderful souls, bursting with wisdom and clad in the rich tapestry of their own stories, yet something remained elusive—a thread that deeply connected all that she had learned about love, warmth, and the importance of nurturing relationships. The key, Mia discovered, lay in the unapologetic embrace of honesty. An encounter with an elder, a sage who had seen the passing of seasons yet remained ever vibrant in spirit, offered her profound insight into the art of truthfulness.

Sitting cross-legged beneath the old oak tree—a venerable witness to laughter and tears—the elder's eyes twinkled with experience. When Mia shared her struggles with communication, the Elder leaned closer, enveloping her in an air of calm assurance. He recounted stories of his own encounters where the pursuit of authenticity led to deepened connections. Each tale wove together the fabric of vulnerability, depicting individuals who risked exposing their innermost thoughts and emotions, and in doing so, created an environment where others felt safe to open up as well. It was as if they played a symphony of shared truths, with each note resonating through the hearts of mutual understanding. The Elder spoke of the times he had feared vulnerability, the anxious stirring in his chest at the thought of unraveling his heart before others, yet it was this very step into authenticity that ultimately felled the barriers forged in insecurity, allowing authentic bonds to blossom.

In the days that followed, Mia began to experiment with the newfound wisdom, predominantly in her interactions with those around her. On a bright morning, filled with the sweet scent of blooming lilacs, she visited the artisan who had so profoundly inspired her as he moulded clay into graceful forms. She recalled lingering moments in the sun-kissed workshop where beautiful creations sprung to life from his hands, imbued with a divine sense of purpose. Welcoming her into his space with a warm smile, the artisan beckoned her to join him at the wheel. As her fingers teamed up with the moist clay, it felt like a visceral representation of the trust that both of them were forging in this moment. Addressing him through this lens of openness, she decided to voice her thoughts—worries mingled with admiration, honesty embraced with a hint of vulnerability. "I feel often that there are things unsaid that hold us apart, yes? Isn't it funny how we create boundaries even when we cherish the connection we have?" The artisan paused, his hands still for a moment before he resumed the dance of creation, responding with a thoughtful nod that encapsulated understanding. "Ah, Mia. To speak honestly is to invite others into the sacred space of one's heart. Truth, my dear, is not merely words; it is the fabric with which we weave our relationships."

Each exchange of authenticity unearthed a new layer of warmth; the connections deepened like the vibrant hues of twilight sky. Mia found herself spilling forth little truths, like the petals of a flower releasing their fragrance on a gentle breeze, revealing fears and joys alike. In gathering her thoughts and presenting them, she discovered the freeing power of honesty. It was not the frail whisper it had once seemed, but rather the strongest force that could unify the bonds between people. With every open-hearted conversation, she opened herself more widely to the vibrancy and intricacies of life, inviting others to share in their own stories and truths. She felt the embrace of trust inching closer, knitting together the souls of those together in authentic connection.

The culmination of her honest endeavours brought about an unexpected celebration within her community—a gathering where diverse faces came to share not just food, laughter, and joy, but an openness to the truths that lived within them, carefully tucked away yet longing to be heard. As the sun dipped low, painting the canvas of the sky in hues of pink and gold, Mia stood before them, her heart pounding with a mix of excitement and vulnerability. Among the cherished friends and newfound companions, she spoke to them—her voice a delicate thread connecting them like a tapestry. They were families, friends, acquaintances, each enriched with their individual struggles and triumphs; she urged them to venture into the golden journey of honesty. "My friends, we often walk around dressed in veils of pretence, like those who wear masks to hide their true selves. Are we not tired of this dance? Let us unmask ourselves tonight. Share your truth, the small joys and the big heartaches, for in sharing, we create an unbreakable bond. No one should walk alone in this world."

One by one, her friends began stepping forth, revealing pieces of their lives that they had long buried beneath layers of expectations. The noise of superficial chatter faded as earnest stories surfaced—baring fears of failure, challenges of heartache, and dreams whispered into the night. Laughter erupted, mingling with teary eyes; the air around them seemed electric with understanding. Within that circle, it was as if they had wrapped a warm quilt around their shoulders, stitched together from the richness of their truths. In that shared vulnerability, Mia felt the weight of pretence lift, and in its place, emerged a heavenly dance of acceptance and love, an unconditional embrace that promised no judgment. Eyes sparkling with recognition, they spoke as one, resonating with the harmonies of unity.

As the evening deepened, the gathering became a home not defined by brick and mortar, but by the authenticity of shared experience and the richness of emotions unfurling like petals blooming into the warm embrace of the sun. Mia sauntered homeward, the moonlight spilling silver streams across her path—a metaphor for the trails of honesty she had illuminated with her burgeoning authenticity. Every step resonated with the power of the truths shared that night, solidifying in her heart that honesty was not merely a trait but a vital force capable of dismantling the walls around her heart and the hearts of those she cherished.

In moments alone, she began to reflect upon her own fears—the fears that had once held her back from speaking her mind, that single fragility that made her hesitate at the threshold of honesty. She acknowledged them now, realizing that it was those same fears that had kept her shackled. Nurtured by the warmth of the encouragement she had found among her friends, Mia sought to build her new truth with love and resilience. In moments of solitude, on quiet evenings by the fireplace, she began to write letters to those she had wronged or misrepresented, sweeping aside the weight of shame in an effort to make amends. As she poured her heart onto the pages, she uncovered the ends of vulnerability and discovered a rejuvenated sense of joy in crafting her own narrative—a story wrapped in love and forgiveness. The act of genuinely communicating transformed her heart, flowing through her like the gentle currents of a nurturing river, revealing the innate beauty of connection.

At last, as days melted into weeks, Mia began to craft her home, not just filled with memories, but enriched with the very essence of truth. Each corner radiated warmth as friends and family came together to build it not with brick and mortar but with spirit and love. They embellished the spaces with laughter, shared meals laden with stories, and music echoing through the air as memories danced all around them. In moments of gathering, Mia felt an inexplicable joy—the knowing that each person who entered her life was a part of this beautiful construct, nurtured from inner honesty and mutual respect. Together, they spun a rich tapestry of existence, woven from courage and empathy, anchoring their hearts with the fundamental truth that true wealth lies not in contingent materialism, but buried deep in the bonds they had forged along the way.

Honesty, once a formidable mountain, became a gentle slope, and Mia savoured the outputs of her journey. The home she had built with words transformed into a sanctuary—a beacon of light for others to find their place. Encounters with past acquaintances turned into lifelong friendships, and familiar faces transformed into priceless connections that would forever enrich her life. The teachings of the elder, the artisan, and the monk pieced together a magnificent truth: there is a wealth more profound than what gleams in the eyes of consumerism, a wealth that adorns the heart, nurtured by the sacred language of honesty and enriched by the love that surrounds them. The journey had brought her to a sacred understanding that a rich home is where the heart is—the heart that was made whole through the rhythm of truth reverberating through every precious room.

8

FRIENDSHIP PALETTE

As Mia strolled through the quaint streets of her town, a gentle breeze wrapped around her, swirling leaves and whispers of connection into her path. Each step felt lighter than the last, as if the weight of the world was being lifted by the newfound radiance within her heart. It was during this time of self-discovery that she began to notice all the vibrant colours of friendship weaving through her life, a palette that promised to enrich the canvas of her existence. The jagged edges that once made her world felt harsh were slowly becoming softened by laughter and the joys of shared experiences. Mia had spent much time introspecting about the nature of love and familial bonds, yet it was now that she was awakening to the diverse shadows and highlights of friendship.

Her first brush with these vivid new relationships occurred at a local art class. Standing before a blank canvas, Mia felt a pang of uncertainty, caught in the liminal space between hesitation and enthusiasm. The room buzzed with laughter, a delightful noise that beckoned her to lean closer, to invest her heart deeper into this experience. She found herself seated next to a woman named Chloe, an effervescent spirit with an abundance of kindness painted across her features. Their conversation unfurled like a blooming flower; as they chatted, Mia learned that Chloe was a single mother who juggled several jobs, yet still found time to pursue her passion for art. The depths of Chloe's life resonated with the melody of resilience, a quality that Mia cherished. In those sentiments, she felt a flicker of hope—a reminder that beauty can emerge from struggle, and friendship can bridge the gaps left by solitude.

Each stroke of the brush became a metaphor, each colour an expression of emotion. As they mixed pigments, they talked about dreams long hidden beneath the dust of everyday obligations. They shared stories of laughter and sorrow; Chloe regaled Mia with tales of mischief from her childhood, while Mia offered snippets of her own narrative of searching for purpose. With each revealing of secrets came a blushing of colours on their canvases and in their hearts. Mia realized that the hues of friendship were intimately tied to those of love. In creating together, they formed a bond that wouldn't soon dull. Laughter echoed in the art room, their shared joy resonating beyond mere companionship; it felt like an intricate dance of souls intertwining. In that vibrant space, a friendship blossomed—a tender shoot reaching toward the sunlight, fuelled by shared passions and mutual understanding.

As weeks turned into months, the bonds deepened among her art class friends, a small community burgeoning in vibrant strokes. Each person contributed their unique voice—an elderly gentleman, whom they affectionately nicknamed 'The Painter of Dreams,' shared wisdom gleaned from decades spent in pursuit of artistic expression. His gentle encouragement taught Mia about vulnerability, the importance of laying bare one's spirit before the world. The camaraderie grew as they would often find themselves critiquing each other's masterpieces, not with judgment but with a loving honesty that rendered their voices inseparable. It is in honesty, Mia would come to learn, where true friendship uncovers its treasure.

With this camaraderie blossoming, Mia also found herself drawn into spontaneous adventures with newfound friends, each an exquisite thread adding to the tapestry of her life. One such adventure was a weekend excursion to the nearby hills. As they hiked leisurely, laughter cascaded amongst them, echoing through the valleys as their footsteps mingled with the rustle of grass and wildflowers. Chloe led the way with her vibrant energy, recounting hilarious moments from their previous week's art class, gesturing dramatically as her friends erupted in laughter. The outline of their friendship became clearer with every shared moment: support, spontaneity, and the joy of the simple things being part of daily life.

Amidst the laughter, Mia could feel the comfort of acceptance enveloping her. Every conversation dipped into new depths, revealing layers previously unseen. An animated young man named Leo, who had an infectious sense of humour and an artistic energy that flowed freely, became another beacon of connection. He often brought aviation-themed jokes that would leave them all giggling, yet it was in his quieter moments that Mia felt a profound connection—a vulnerability that resonated within. It was as if they were painting vibrant portraits of connection, heedless of conventional boundaries, yet with utmost care for the strokes shared between them.

Over coffees and flaky pastries, the conversations transitioned from the whimsical to the heartfelt, moving toward discussions about dreams, failures, aspirations, and fears. They explored their narratives with grace, embracing the vulnerability submerged in personal stories, echoing what Mia felt within her soul—it was a grace that transcended the superficial chatter of acquaintances. Through this warmth of friendship, Mia began to embrace her own beautiful imperfections, discovering shades of herself previously undiscovered.

But it was at an unexpected moment of quiet, nestled in the

charm of a small café, that a transformative shift occurred within Mia. She found herself in deep conversation with an elderly woman, an art enthusiast who had just stepped into the cafe after a gallery tour. This woman, whose name was Eliza, painted the vivid stories of her life in a palette of wisdom and experience. As Mia listened, she felt something resonate deep within her, realizing that each person she met painted their own layer onto her heart's canvas. Eliza spoke of the friendships she had forged through the years, friendships that weathered seasons, ones that were forged from shared struggles and laughter, emphasizing how each connection had fortified her spirit.

Inspired, Mia found herself reflecting on the multicultural richness of their conversations, realizing that each friend, with their unique backgrounds and stories, brought forth a new hue to her life. It was not just about her initial pursuit of love and family; it was about weaving together the many colours that friendships offered—a kaleidoscope emerging from individual stories. It filled her heart with warmth to know that these friendships would only deepen with time, nurturing her soul and expanding her understanding of affection beyond the confines of familial love.

The days spent with her friends continued to bloom like unfolding petals, carrying their own fragrance of attachment and loyalty. Mia soon became adept at balancing her chaotic life while embracing the warmth of her community. Her heart swelled with gratitude for the tapestry of friendship that now adorned her life so beautifully. In moments of silence, reflective walks after art class, or cozy evenings spent reminiscing over shared meals, Mia felt the bond of companionship surge. It was in these moments that she grasped the spectrum of love that existed between companions—a vivid spectrum where trust and kindness twined together, forming something far richer than mere moments of joy.

As she engaged more deeply with her friends, a realization tugged at Mia: a rich home arises from the shared warmth and support woven between people walking alongside each other. She began to perceive the intricacies of companionship—the vulnerability, laughter, shared truths, and solemnity mingling together to create a sanctuary from life's storms. It was this understanding that became the lens through which she viewed love: as not merely an emotion confined to familial ties or romantic entanglements, but as a broad, brilliant spectrum painted by the hands of many.

Mia came to appreciate that proximity did not solely define a connection. Instead, it was the shared moments and mutual growth that built lasting foundations for friendships. In embracing this notion, she found a kinship with her friends that transcended daily interactions. Together, they nurtured each other's dreams and passions, lifting one another with unwavering belief, forming a supportive network that blossomed within the rich soil of honesty and kindness. Each friend contributed to building this beautiful sanctuary that housed the essence of a rich home, the emotional connections creating vibrations that resonated like soft music in the hearts of each.

As she lay beneath the embrace of the stars one evening during a laid-back gathering in the park, Mia reflected on how monumental this chapter had been in her life. She could feel the warmth of smiles around her, her friends lost in laughter, their energy kaleidoscopic against the backdrop of the dark sky. The brilliance of friendship surrounded Mia like a comforting hug, a refuge that encouraged growth and exploration. As she ventured forth on her journey, she was encouraged to let love flow, to give generously of herself, and most importantly, to bloom alongside those who would help her experience the richness of life. Thus, Mia stepped into the sunlight of friendship, a vibrant kaleidoscope illuminating the path toward her beloved home, ever enriched by the colourful palettes now adorning her heart.

9

LOVE IN ACTION

As Mia walked through the heart of her bustling community, she found herself enveloped in a tapestry of emotions that showcased the essence of love in action. The sun hung low in the afternoon sky, casting a warm golden hue upon the streets, and it felt as though the very air was imbued with the aroma of connection and kindness. Observing the interactions around her, Mia noted the familial love emanating from a nearby park, where a mother, with laughter bubbling in her voice, chased after her children as they darted between swings and slides. She could feel the energy of delight radiating from the family as they played together, the children's laughter ringing like a melodious echo in her heart. Each moment she witnessed was a paint stroke on the expansive canvas of love, reminding her of the sacred bond shared between a parent and child, one built on trust, care, and an unwavering support system that served as an anchor even in the stormiest of seas.

Pausing to absorb the scene, Mia noticed another family nearby—a grandmother, her hands weathered yet gentle, was sharing stories with her grandchildren. They clamoured around her, eyes wide with wonder, as she animatedly recounted tales of their ancestry, weaving threads of history into the fabric of their lives. Their giggles and exclamations transformed her stories into a river of shared thoughts and emotions, flowing seamlessly from one generation to the next. Mia's heart swelled with a longing to connect with such warmth, to deluge herself in the richness of her own roots, illuminating the unique hues of her family history that had shaped the woman she was becoming.

As Mia continued her exploration, she stumbled upon a group of friends gathered around a small coffee shop, their laughter spilling out into the street. They conversed freely, engaging in animated discussions that echoed the cadence of their shared experiences. Observing the camaraderie from a distance, Mia couldn't help but admire how their friendship served as a haven of solace and joy. The way they bantered playfully, shared secrets that carried whispers of trust, and offered encouragement showed her that friendship held a unique shade of love, a bond that relied not just on familiarity but on a mutual understanding and respect. It reaffirmed her belief that love was not confined to blood relations; rather, it was fluid and vital, taking shape in myriad forms, enriching lives and deepening connections.

With every step she took, Mia's perception expanded further to include the neighbours who gathered on their porches, exchanging laughter and stories while sipping lemonade. From one porch to another, she could see the shared meals, the helping hands extended during moments of trouble, and the unspoken solidarity that proved how love emanated in simple, beautiful gestures. It was as if each neighbourhood gathering was a sacred ritual, drawing together the individuals into a web of shared humanity. These glimpses of everyday life stirred something profound within her, igniting a flame that flickered with hope and encouraged her to explore her own capacity to love and connect.

Mia's journey led her deeper into a neighbourhood festival, where the community came alive with vibrancy and festivity, a vibrant celebration held beneath shimmering lanterns fluttering like butterflies in the warm breeze. The local park had transformed into a mosaic of life that day, bustling with families gathered for the annual community festival. Laughter adorned the air like the sweet scent of blooming flowers, and the vibrant colours of balloons danced amidst the golden rays of sunlight. Children darted about, their carefree giggles a stark contrast to the whispers of sadness that had shadowed Mia for far too long. For once, she felt a rush of hope glimmering in her chest, an undisguised yearning for connection that seemed to resonate with the very rhythm of the celebration. She found herself drawn to a long table adorned with dishes bursting with culinary delights, each one a story of tradition and love patiently crafted by the hands of the community's home cooks. As she folded her arms and gazed longingly at the spread, she felt the tug of hunger—not just of the body, but of the heart—a longing for togetherness that had eluded her for so long.

It was while she was lost in thought that an elderly woman, her silver hair shimmering in the light, approached Mia with a welcoming smile that seemed to radiate warmth. "Would you care to share a dish?" she asked, her eyes twinkling with kindness. Mia felt a sudden rush of gratitude wash over her; an emotion she scarcely remembered feeling. "I'd love to," she replied, a smile breaking across her face with a spontaneity that surprised even her. The elderly woman led her to the table, where they stood together, sampling the rich flavours prepared by others who had gathered in the same spirit of camaraderie. As they shared stories about their culinary conquests—the art of baking bread, the secret to perfectly spiced lentil soup—Mia lost herself in a dialogue that flowed as freely as the fragrant lemonade that filled their cups.

Throughout the festival, she encountered a myriad of individuals, each carrying with them their unique essence, adding layers to her understanding of what it meant to belong. There was Sam, a quirky artist whose laughter could brighten even the darkest of days, and Yasmin, a single mother whose resilience breathed life into the very air they shared. Through conversations that brimmed with authenticity, she began to piece together their diverse stories, weaving them closely into her own narrative. Each interaction felt like a brushstroke, painting her life anew with colours she had once confined to the background.

With each anecdote shared, Mia felt a bridge forming over the chasm of loneliness she had carried with her. The warmth of belonging wrapped around her like a soft blanket on a chilly night. As the sun dipped lower in the sky, casting golden hues across the grassy knoll, she noticed families settling under trees, blankets sprawled out like colourful quilts of community. They invited her to join them, a sense of inclusion dancing in the air as they exchanged laughter and tales of their daily lives. What once felt like an insurmountable disconnect transformed into a shared sense of experience, the blending of stories echoing in the hearts of those seated together.

Amidst the festival's vibrant energy, she noticed a group sitting quietly at a small table, their mission not as boisterous as the celebrations around them yet equally powerful. They were creating care packages for the less fortunate within their community, and Mia felt her heart swell as she witnessed love in action—love that was expressed without the expectation of anything in return. These individuals showcased what it meant to cultivate compassion in practical ways, demonstrating how care could manifest through genuine actions that upheld the dignity of every person. Watching them work together with laughter and familiarity warmed her soul, solidifying her understanding that love could serve as the dormant seed of change that could transform lives in unexpected ways.

That evening, the melodies of local musicians serenaded the attendees, filling the park with songs that transcended language and culture. Mia found herself swaying gently, the music merging with the palpable spirit of community that surrounded her, each note strumming a chord in her heart that resonated with hope. One particular musician struck a chord with her; his soulful words resonated deeply, speaking of love lost and found, of experiences that shaped hearts. He poured every ounce of his being into the performance, captivating the audience and eliciting a collective sigh of recognition. In that moment, Mia discovered that love could also find voice through art, echoing the stories of countless souls who yearned for connection. The melodies encapsulated not only joy but sorrow, intertwining both into a universal language that called to her spirit, urging her to honour the fears and hopes that echoed within her heart, prompting a longing for expression. Little by little, she found herself letting go of her isolation, embracing the common humanity that connected them all. With every song sung, she felt her heart expand, allowing joy to seep into the cracks that once drove her apart from the collective tapestry of community life.

As twilight descended, Mia reflected on the myriad forms love had taken throughout her journey. Every act she had witnessed expanded her understanding of what it meant to cultivate a rich home, a haven not of material abundance but of emotional depth and connection. She came to realize that love twisted and flowed like a river, nourishing and enlivening everything it touched—families enriched their homes with care and laughter, friendships constructed safe harbours built on trust, while acts of kindness painted a community with warmth and compassion. This realization unfurled like the petals of a flower within her heart, awakening a desire to create her own legacy of love, for she now understood that home was not merely a place, but a consciously curated experience shaped by the compassion and authenticity she chose to embody.

Filled with newfound inspiration, Mia began to dream of her own abundant future, where she would infuse her life with the lessons she had gleaned from her observations. Love in action became the mantra that reverberated in her mind, compelling her to not just seek relationships that made her feel whole, but to give love freely, nurturing the bonds that had been so richly demonstrated around her. It was then, within this torrent of realizations, that she promised herself she would walk forth into the world, hugging every facet of love close to her heart, becoming a vessel for warmth and light amid the vast tapestry of humanity. The journey of understanding had only just begun, and she was more than ready to embrace the beautiful simplicity of love and transform it into a legacy that transcended time, entwining her soul with those she would meet along the way, painting her existence with the richest colours of connection, trust, and warmth.

10

TOGETHER IN HARMONY

Mia had always imagined community as a distant concept, one that existed in the echoes of her childhood, a place where bonds were forged and laughter mingled with the aroma of shared meals. Yet, until now, it had merely been a figment of her imagination, a portrait painted in the colourful hues of nostalgia. It was only when she began to truly step out of her shell, turning her thoughts away from the confines of her solitary world, that she felt the seductive pull of community life. Under the warm glow of the sun, she walked to the heart of her neighbourhood, her senses alive with the vibrant tapestry of humanity that unfolded around her.

As she strolled home under a canopy of stars, Mia held her heart high with a newfound lightness, a realization swirling within her: she was indeed a part of something far greater than herself. The connections she had fostered, the stories exchanged, and the laughter shared were not just fleeting moments, but seeds planted in the fertile soil of community. They would grow and blossom, creating a sanctuary rich in love, trust, and acceptance. Her footsteps, once heavy with doubt and despair, now echoed affirmatively against the pavement, affirming her embrace of community life.

In these moments of togetherness, Mia found the very essence of what she had been searching for all along. The warmth she craved enveloped her, a robust tapestry woven from her family's memories and the lives of those around her. The festival, a catalyst of change, became a reminder that in unity lies unwavering strength, illuminating her path towards a home brimming with the treasures of love and togetherness, real treasures that made the heart beam with joy.

11

THE CIRCLE OF FRIENDS

In the chapters of Mia's life, a profound realization dawned upon her, much like the gentle light of dawn piercing through the darkness of night. It was during her pursuit of what truly constituted a rich home that she began to understand the invaluable essence of companionship and communal bonds. The circle of friends began to take shape as she ventured into the tapestry of life, each thread intertwining to create an intricate pattern of togetherness, warmth, and unwavering support. Mia had always moved through the world with a sense of solitude, often encased in a bubble that felt more isolating than protective. Her previous endeavours, marked by material accumulation, proved to be but fleeting distractions, failing to satiate the deep-seated yearnings of her heart. It was only through the serendipitous encounters of her journey that she recognized the significance of genuine relationships—those forged in authenticity and trust, blooming beautifully in the soil of shared experiences.

Her path led her to a quaint café nestled in a corner of a busy street, where the air was alive with the laughter of patrons and the aroma of freshly brewed coffee mingled with the sweet scent of pastries. It was there, among the clinking of cups and the murmur of conversations, that she first connected with Sam, a spirited artist with a heart as vibrant as the canvases he filled with colour. As they shared a table under the warm glow of sunlight streaming through the window, Mia felt a spark ignite—a sense of kinship that washed over her like the gentle waves of the ocean caressing the shore. Sam enchanted her with his stories of creating art not just for the sake of beauty, but rather as a means of expressing the deep emotions that often remained unspoken. Their conversations danced from laughter to introspection, and Mia found herself divulging personal anecdotes with an openness she'd never imagined possible. In Sam, she discovered a friend who not only understood the melodrama of human existence but celebrated it through the lens of creativity. This newfound friendship blossomed, paving the way for further connections that would enrich Mia's life in remarkable ways.

Mia's circle began to expand, each new friend adding a unique hue to the vibrant tapestry she was weaving. She soon crossed paths with Anaya, whose laughter rang like music through the air, effortlessly inviting those around her into her overflowing well of joy. Anaya had a gift for cultivating happiness, bringing together people from all walks of life, uniting them in a spirit of camaraderie that illuminated even the darkest corners of doubt. Mia often marvelled at how Anaya could effortlessly transform mundane gatherings into illuminating celebrations of life, where friendships flourished like wildflowers in spring. It was through Anaya's lens that Mia first glimpsed the profound impact of shared joy.

The circle of friends enveloped Mia, providing a support system that was both nurturing and empowering. Among the group emerged Ethan, a reflective soul with a passion for music. He serenaded them with melodies that echoed the varied facets of life, each note portraying stories of love, loss, laughter, and resilience. Mia listened, enchanted by the way music painted emotions with each strum of his guitar. In Ethan's songs, she discovered the universal language that binds humanity together, transcending boundaries and uniting hearts in the beautiful rhythm of existence. His ability to capture the essence of friendships in his lyrics resonated deeply within her, further emphasizing the importance of the bonds they were creating. Together, these friendships formed an unbreakable circle—a safe haven where Mia felt instant solace, a refuge from the chaos of her outer world. As they explored the beauty of life through shared adventures, Mia began to weave pieces of herself into the narratives of her friends, embracing their joys and sorrows as though they were her own.

In moments of vulnerability, each friend offered a listening ear, a shoulder to cry on, or simply a comforting presence. Mia recalled times when doubts whispered insidiously into her mind, challenging her newfound vision of a rich life. Yet, in those moments, surrounded by her friends, she felt the warmth of togetherness wrap tightly around her, dispelling the chilling grip of uncertainty. Their encouragement became a lifeline, reaffirming her quest as a noble and worthy pursuit, fuelling the fire within her to chase after something transcendent. Together, they celebrated each personal milestone, transforming small victories into monumental tributes to their growing bond. Each shared experience fortified the foundation of trust and intimacy, laying down roots that would weather the test of time.

Through her interactions within this circle, Mia encountered diverse perspectives that illuminated her understanding of what it meant to live a rich life. Her friends had different histories, experiences that shaped their unique outlooks on the world, each beckoning her to see beyond her own narrative. Through deep conversations filled with curiosity and respect, they shared lessons that reverberated through her being. There was Sam, whose artistic musings inspired her to look at life through a kaleidoscope of emotions, while Anaya's outright zest provoked her to revel in the sweetness surrounding every moment. Ethan, with his songs, provided an anthem to the collective spirit of their friendships—an endless tribute to the symphony they were composing together.

As seasons changed, so too did the nature of her circle. The bonds grew stronger through shared trials and jubilations, pointing Mia toward the ultimate truth she had long sought: a true home thrives in the warmth of unconditionally loving relationships. It was during a stormy evening, with rain drumming fiercely against the window, that their circle shimmered the brightest. As they gathered at Mia's house, the atmosphere crackled with warmth—their laughter intermingling with the sound of rain, resonating within the walls like a heartbeat. They huddled together, exchanging stories wrapped in humour, sharing past experiences that brought tears of laughter, each anecdote threading them closer to one another.

In the hush that followed the cacophony of laughter, Mia unveiled her vulnerability, sharing her fears and her longing for a place where she could belong. As she articulated her dreams, the silence was soft yet palpable; her friends held their breath in reverence, allowing the weight of her words to settle like a cherished blessing among them. In that sacred moment, the circle of friends formed a tapestry of empathy and understanding, offering words of encouragement that wrapped around Mia like a soothing balm. They assured her she was not alone, expressing how they believed fiercely in her dreams, each voice a powerful affirmation that bolstered her spirit. In that room, amid the flickering candlelight, Mia felt embraced by the kind of love she had yearned for all along—the kind of love that could never be torn asunder, even by the harsh winds of the outside world.

Each amiable face surrounding her became a reflection of the beauty she sought, and as she immersed herself in the flow of their shared existence, she discovered the unyielding power of community that permeated each facet of life. Together, they became architects of a profound vision—a home enriched not just by physical space but by an unwavering dedication to one another's growth and happiness.

In the weeks that followed, as the sun continued to rise and set, illuminating their lives, the circle of friends thrived. The bonds they forged grew not just in strength, but in depth, allowing Mia to explore the compelling tapestry of her truth. Time spent together blossomed into precious rituals, from storytelling nights to shared meals, where laughter echoed and tears flowed freely—a beautiful symphony of the human experience. Each moment they created together served as a brick laid upon the foundation of the rich home Mia had envisioned, the kind of abode that fostered peace, love, and joy. Each gathering complemented how they saw the world—an exquisite kaleidoscope bursting with colours of generosity, trust, and empathy, reflecting the depth of their bonds back to one another with every passing day.

As the sunlight cast warm hues through the windows of her life, filling the corners of her heart, Mia could sense that in nurturing these friendships—her circle of friends—she was cultivating the very essence of what it meant to feel at home. With every passing moment, the echoes of laughter, tenderness, and heartfelt trust intertwined like a harmonious melody, capturing the beauty of human connection in its fullest form. Through the dance of their lives, amidst the vibrant tapestry woven between them, she discovered that within the love they shared, she had finally found the rich home she had long sought—a true sanctuary of the heart, transcending the limits of material wealth and echoing with the priceless treasures tucked within the essence of each cherished bond. Each friend illuminating her journey was akin to stars against the night sky: unique, radiant, and forever reminding Mia that she never had to walk alone. Together, they would continue to create a rich legacy of love, nurturing their hearts and connections through a tapestry that would endure across lifetimes, forever cultivating a sanctuary built not upon wealth, but upon the richness of mutual respect, understanding, and love.

12

THE HEART OF TOGETHERNESS

The sun dipped low on the horizon, casting a golden hue that embraced the small village where Mia had begun to find her footing, a village that pulsed with life and laughter. In the centre of this vibrant tapestry stood a large, ancient oak tree, its branches stretching outward as if in a perpetual gesture of welcome, a sentinel of memories and conversations shared beneath its canopy. It was here that Mia, buoyed by her burgeoning understanding of what made a home truly rich, decided to organize a festival, a celebration that would bring together the diverse threads of the community she had slowly begun to unravel. With each passing day, she had felt the joys of togetherness seep into her soul, wrapping her in warmth like a thick, comfortable quilt. The enthusiasm for this festival sparked life into the hearts of her neighbours as they shared their hopes and fears, weaving a tapestry of vulnerability and affection that spilled into every corner of the community.

As preparations began, the aroma of freshly baked bread mingled with the cheerful sounds of children playing and the rhythmic clattering of pots and pans filled the air. This was not just a gathering of bodies; it was a wholehearted embracing of spirits. The women of the village, fuelled by their love for one another and the shared desire to celebrate the bonds that held them together, transformed the central square into a feast for the senses. Vibrant flowers adorned tables, their colours reflecting the joy and heart of each individual who contributed their time and skills. Old stories were shared, laden with laughter and the kind of deep care that only comes from years of knowing one another. Mia wandered among them, her heart swelling as she witnessed the simple acts of connection—hands reaching out to help, words of encouragement exchanged over steaming bowls of stew, and the melodies of soulful songs weaving through the air, rich with history and emotion.

On the day of the festival, the atmosphere pulsated with a different kind of energy; it was a celebration of lives intertwined, a celebration of the strength found in unity. From afar, Mia watched as her neighbours, some she'd barely spoken to just weeks prior, now embraced one another as if they were long-lost kin. She could see the older generations sharing the wisdom of their experiences, while the younger folk listened with rapt attention, threading their own dreams and aspirations into the fabric of shared laughter. It became evident to her that this gathering was not just about food or festivities, but rather an affirmation of the strength of interdependence, a lesson that resonated with a profound clarity in her heart. The spirit of togetherness manifested itself in shared stories, communal efforts, and a collective sense of belonging, transcending the superficial barriers that often-kept people at arm's length.

As evening approached, lanterns hung from the branches of the great oak, casting a soft glow that felt magical and ethereal. Mia felt the pulsating heartbeat of her community resonate through the air, a gentle reminder that togetherness was not simply a word, but a vibrant force that needed nurturing. She took to her place beneath the oak, her heart a blend of nerves and excitement. With every soul surrounding her, she understood that this was far more than a festival; it was a testament to the human spirit, a vibrant declaration of love that sought to champion unity over discord. The laughter of children rang out like the sweetest symphony, breaking through the invisible walls many had built around themselves, as the music began to play, transcending language, age, and culture. Couples danced, their movements fluid and joyous, while friends clapped in rhythm, creating a melody of harmony that echoed through the woodlands—a paintbrush to the canvas of a perfect evening.

At the heart of this festival was a potluck dinner, where every participant brought a dish that told a story, a glimpse into their hearts, each culinary creation forming a mosaic of flavours and emotions. As Mia tasted these offerings, the simple ingredients revealed complex histories; each bite was infused with memories, hopes, and love. The artisan, who had once shaped small pieces of clay turned to creating tortillas for the gathering, spoke passionately about the way food linked generations, each recipe passed down gifting a sense of continuity and belonging. Mia listened intently, her heart swelled with admiration for this wise potter who, in teaching her about his craft, revealed the beauty of the intertwined lives that formed the community. They were all artisans crafting their narratives, binding themselves to one another through gestures of kindness, shared meals, and above all, upholding the essence of trust and love.

And as twilight deepened, Mia felt a profound shift within herself. Fuelled by connection, she stepped forward to share her own story, a kaleidoscope of emotions as she spoke of her journey, the dim echoes of her loneliness contrasting with the resounding harmony of now. Her voice trembled with vulnerability, yet it reflected a burgeoning strength as she narrated the richness she discovered within these connections that flourished like wildflowers, defying the constraints of time and circumstance. Back in her former life, she had been surrounded by opulent luxuries, but here, among these incredible souls, she had discovered a wealth unfathomable in its depth. It was in the laughter of friends, the genuine concern of neighbours, and the love that permeated even the simplest of moments—a richness so intense it buffered against her past, allowing her to reconcile with who she was and who she wanted to become.

As she ended her story, silence enveloped the gathering, an unspoken understanding woven through the attendees like an intricate tapestry. Then, one by one, voices began to rise, each person sharing their experiences, their challenges, their dreams. As the circle of vulnerability expanded, Mia's heart danced joyfully at the realization that amidst life's ebbs and flows, they had built a fortress of unity, the branches of which would forever shelter them through life's storms. Tears glistened in eyes not just from grief, but with gratitude, for it was within this manifestation of togetherness that healing began. The vibrant energy pulsated within the crowd, mirroring the beating heart of the village itself—a heartbeat that resonated with love, hope, and an unwavering commitment to nurture the connections that had blossomed.

As the festival drew to a close, the lanterns flickered like the stars in the night sky, illuminating paths for the myriad of tiny, yet powerful, connections that had been enriched and renewed under the watchful gaze of the oak tree. Mia stood among her neighbours, her heart overflowing with gratitude, an eternal reminder that this rich home—a home that transcended the physical limitations of her ancestral abode—had been built right here, among the laughter, stories, and heartbeats of those gathered around her. In that moment, she envisioned the walls of her family's home adorned with the echoes of conversations shared and bonds formed, a living testament to the richness generated by love and unity. From now on, that home would not be merely a building; it would operate as a sanctuary of warmth, the cornerstone of which was the cherished community she had come to embrace. The gift of togetherness was her legacy, gifting her a life intertwined with others along the beautiful tapestry of being human—each thread shimmering with shared history, love, and an unwavering belief in the strength found when hearts unite.

13

THE SPIRIT OF GENEROSITY

Mia stood before the entrance of the local community centre, her heart pounding, not from anxiety but from the thrill of new beginnings. This was not her first time volunteering, but each experience had painted a vivid portrait of the world's beauty, intricately woven with the threads of kindness and community spirit. Today, she was eager to embrace this opportunity. The faded paint and weathered bricks of the building spoke of countless stories, and Mia felt a strange comfort in knowing that her presence would soon contribute to a narrative full of warmth and connection. Equipped with a generous heart and a desire to serve, she stepped inside, ready to engage in a journey that would touch not only those around her but also profoundly reshape her understanding of fulfilment.

As Mia first entered the bustling hall, the scent of freshly baked bread enveloped her, mingling with laughter and the warm camaraderie of individuals from diverse backgrounds. She was welcomed by the enthusiastic coordinator, Anna, whose eyes sparkled with compassion and a genuine love for the community she served. Anna explained the day's activities: organizing a food drive, preparing care packages, and facilitating workshops for children in need. Each task felt like a small stitch in the larger tapestry of humanity, and Mia could feel her spirit soar as she grabbed an apron and joined the flurry of activity.

Working alongside others ignited a flicker of joy within her; the inviting smiles exchanged were like luminous threads, weaving connections that enriched her life. With each passing hour, Mia immersed herself in the rhythm of service, her hands busily assembling packets of food and essential items. With every can of soup she placed, she envisioned the warmth of a home filled not just with belongings but with love. Children scampered about the room, giggling excitedly as they crafted colourful drawings and messages that would accompany the care packages, each scribble echoing the heartfelt sentiments of generosity and hope.

As the day wore on, Mia thoughtfully observed the interactions around her. She learned from the elderly volunteers who regaled her with stories of their past, sharing experiences that spoke of resilience, kindness, and community support during their most trying times. Each tale added brushstrokes to the vivid canvas she was beginning to understand—how true wealth isn't counted in monetary figures but rather felt in the depth of the connections we forge through selfless acts. She began to recognize the collective heartbeat of the community, a rhythm pulsing with shared history, challenges, and triumphs, each individual a vital note in this harmonious symphony.

By mid-afternoon, the atmosphere crackled with excitement as they prepared for the workshop with the children. Mia had been assigned to lead an arts and crafts session, her heartbeat resonating with anticipation and purpose. She watched as youthful faces transformed into portraits of curiosity and creativity, each child overflowing with boundless imagination. Guided by their laughter, she encouraged them to express themselves, watching joy unfold within their strokes of paint and glitter. Among them, a shy girl named Lila caught Mia's attention, her hesitant hands trembling as they grasped the brush. With gentle encouragement, Mia guided her, and as they painted side by side, vibrant colours began to emerge upon the canvas—a reflection not only of Lila's artistic spirit but also a blossoming friendship that transcended the confines of their circumstances.

Through the laughter and gleeful chatter, Mia discovered the healing power of heartfelt connection. Each sincere smile shared, every compliment exchanged, and every moment spent together reaffirmed her understanding of home. It was no longer just a physical space but a collection of intertwined lives rich in emotional wealth. Later that evening, as the volunteers served hot meals to families streaming in, Mia felt her heart swell with a sense of fulfilment she had long been searching for. The gratitude radiating from those she served was a profound reminder of the impact small acts of kindness could ripple across lives. Each smile felt like a sprinkle of light in her own spirit, illuminating the essence of humanity's enduring capacity for love.

After the day concluded, Mia lingered in the now-quiet community centre, taking a moment to soak it all in. The walls, once simply mere structures, now pulsed with the vibrant energy of connection. She thought of Lila and her new friends—not just as children she had met for a fleeting moment, but as threads in the fabric of her life, woven together through the shared endeavour of serving and uplifting one another. Mia envisioned a kaleidoscope of interactions that expanded in her mind, a beautiful representation of how kindness creates endearing bonds, empowering both giver and receiver.

As she walked home that evening, the setting sun painted the sky in shades of orange and pink, echoing the warmth she had witnessed in the community. Mia felt the weight of solitude lift as a sense of belonging took its place. The rich tapestry of interactions she had woven would be the foundation of her own home, defined not by material goods but by the heart's ability to connect, serve, and uplift others. The fulfilment she had craved blossomed within her, transforming her view of her surroundings. Each neighbourhood corner, each store, even the simplest park bench now resonated with life waiting to be embraced.

In the days and weeks that followed, Mia continued to volunteer, each session nurturing her spirit and enriching her understanding. She realized that with every laugh shared and story told, she also learned to love herself deeper, gaining a sense of purpose that transcended the physicality of a home. The bonds formed in those hours—built on trust, solidarity, and the joy of giving—were among the greatest treasures she would ever accumulate. The richness of her experiences became her sanctuary, a testament to the power of kindness that transcended the barriers of wealth.

Mia's heart brimmed with gratitude, and as she continued to pour herself into acts of kindness, she was constantly reminded that a rich home is born from the love shared between souls and the connections made along the journey. No longer did she seek a lavish dwelling; her desires had shifted to encompass a home filled with the laughter of friends, regional flavours from shared meals, and the warmth of community gatherings. In her quest, Mia found not just fulfilment but the profound realization that every smile shared, every hand held in service, and every conversation born from humility and empathy stitched together the most beautiful home—the one made everlasting by gifts from the heart.

14

SHARING STORIES

In a small, sun-drenched square where the laughter of children danced on the gentle breeze, Mia found herself immersed in the vibrancy of her community. They had come together for what was becoming a cherished tradition—a gathering known as the Evening of Tales. The informal yet heartfelt event was an embodiment of connection and belonging; it was an occasion where individuals from different walks of life converged, bringing with them the unique tapestry of their stories. On the weathered benches that lined the square, neighbours, friends, and newcomers nestled together, their hearts open and their spirits alive with anticipation.

As dusk settled over the horizon, painting the sky in hues of lavender and gold, Mia took her seat, her heart fluttering with excitement. She had grown to cherish these moments, recognizing that they held the potential to intertwine lives and destinies, sparking a profound understanding of one another through the universal language of storytelling. Each story shared was a brushstroke on the grand canvas of their community, and tonight, she was eager to contribute her own hues, to unveil her narrative and share in the collective heartbeat that resonated from the crowd.

The air buzzed with chatter and laughter, the warmth of companionship enveloping everyone present. Mia listened intently as the first storyteller stepped forward, an elderly woman named Mila, her hair a cascade of silver, shimmering like a beacon in the fading light. Mila's voice, though soft, carried the weight of years and the wisdom they had bestowed upon her, narrating tales of resilience and hope. She spoke of her childhood during a time of unrest, of how her family had forged bonds that no adversity could break. With each word, she spun a web of connection that ensnared the listeners, transporting them to a simpler time where warmth and kindness were the currency of the day. Mia felt the pull of enthusiasm, nodding along with the crowd, realizing how kindness had continued to intertwine their lives throughout generations.

After Mila finished, the applause washed over her like a gentle wave, signifying not just appreciation, but a shared sense of complicity within the community. Mia felt a warmth budding in her chest, an understanding that kindness was more than an isolated act; it was a binding agent that created ties between hearts. Then it was Mark's turn, a young man bursting with energy. He stood tall and confident, radiating an infectious enthusiasm that lit up the room. Mark relayed a story from his college days, detailing how a simple act—a moment spent helping a stranger find their way—had turned into an enduring friendship, a lifelong bond, which continually enriched his life. The laughter that erupted from the crowd during parts of his narrative seemed to weave deeper connections among the listeners, tying them in the warmth of shared humour. Mia couldn't help but smile, as she recognized herself in this tale, recalling her own moments of connection, the little gestures that seemed insignificant but were etched deep into the annals of her spirit.

As the night progressed, various members of the community stepped forward to share their tales—of love lost and found, of dreams tethered to reality, and of the beautiful, messy process of growing together. Each speaker brought forth a piece of their soul, and Mia found herself captivated by the myriad of experiences laid bare before her. An old man named Joseph shared a poignant story about losing his wife; his voice trembled as he conveyed the depths of his loneliness. Yet, woven into the fabric of his grief were the countless acts of kindness he received from his neighbours, hands ready to lend support, meals shared at his doorstep, reminding him that love transcends even the deepest voids. There was a sombre hush that fell over the crowd, a collective heartbeat echoing Joseph's pain, followed by a resounding wave of applause that washed over him, honouring his vulnerability.

And then came Clara, a single mother who spoke of triumph amid trials, her powerful words igniting hope where despair would often linger. She recounted the lowest moments of her life—the struggles of juggling work and parenting alone—but punctuated her tale with gratitude for the support she received. The community rallied around her, offering not just tangible help, but a sanctuary of emotional strength. Mia felt an overwhelming sense of camaraderie—the realization that these stories were not singular; they were threads woven into the collective identity of their neighbourhood. Clara's children burst into the square, their laughter infecting the sombre canvas of evening with an exuberance that echoed through the souls of those adults who sat entranced by her narrative.

As the sun finally dipped below the horizon, giving way to a sky littered with stars that twinkled like diamonds, Mia felt the weight of the evening enveloping her in warmth. She could hardly contain her anticipation—it was her time to share her story. The journey she had undergone to redefine her understanding of home felt intricately tied to the tales she had just heard. With a heart full of gratitude and humble nervousness, she rose to her feet as the gentle evening breeze tousled her hair. Stepping forward, she captured the attention of her community, her spirit igniting the warm glow of the lanterns around them.

Mia began with her own tale, the narrative of her search for a rich home—not one built on material wealth but resting upon a foundation of love and connection. She painted vivid images of her life in lavish surfaces and empty rooms, where echoes of laughter were nothing more than distant memories. Her voice trembled slightly as she recounted the hollow feeling of navigating through luxury without companionship, the yearning for genuine warmth, for bonds that would fill the spaces where silence lingered. She shared how each encounter with the wise Artisan and the contemplative Monk had shaped her understanding, helping her shed the conventional notions of wealth that society had imposed upon her.

As her story unfolded, Mia's eyes sparkled with the thrill of revealing her newfound understanding—how the gravity of community had pulled her back from the edge of disillusionment. She spoke of fleeting moments that captivated her heart—a neighbour's kindness in times of need, the shared laughter with her new friends, and the sanctuary she discovered among those who embraced authenticity. Each anecdote infused with humour and emotion, drew the audience closer, creating a mosaic of connections that illuminated the square against the night sky. When she shared the profound revelation of her cherished ancestral home, her beloved family legacy waiting to be reclaimed, an audible gasp swept through the crowd, reverberating the spirit of unity binding them together.

As Mia concluded her story, a silence filled the air, and then an eruption of applause broke through, washing over her like a wave. The warmth of their hearts enveloped her, assuring her that she had become part of this intricate tapestry of connection, woven together by threads of kindness, trust, and honesty. The Evening of Tales had not just been a simple gathering but a reaffirmation of their bonds; a rich reminder that home wasn't a destination but rather the relationships they cultivated along the way. It was the moments that echoed within them long after the stories were shared, and as they all settled into comfortable camaraderie under the starry sky, Mia felt a profound sense of belonging, a realization that she had found her home, already paid for, filled with love and immeasurable wealth. In that magical evening, the richness of their shared stories entwined their lives, echoing in the very essence of who they were as a community, igniting a hope that would linger and grow for seasons to come.

15

THE RIPPLE EFFECT

As Mia continued her exploration of what constituted true richness, she found herself increasingly captivated by the concept of generosity. It was fascinating how a seemingly simple act of giving, whether in spirit or in deed, could create ripples across the lives of others. This understanding blossomed within her one afternoon while she sat in the orchard, surrounded by fruit trees heavy with golden apples and fragrant blossoms swaying gently in the breeze. As she plucked a ripe apple from its branch, she couldn't help but be reminded of the elderly Artisan she had met earlier in her journey. He had shared stories of how each of his creations—those beautiful, hand-crafted pots—was infused with not just clay but love. He spoke of how each pot, once it left his hands, bore the touch of a heart willing to share and connect. Mia realized then that generosity wasn't confined to grand gestures; it manifested in small, deliberate actions that resonated deeply within the community. It was the elderly neighbour who baked cookies for the local children, her warmth echoing through laughter and smiles. It was the gentle encouragement of a mentor who believed in nurturing the strength of others without expectation.

Mia began to reflect on the ways she had opened her heart to generosity and how those instances had multiplied like dominoes set in motion. She recalled a time when she volunteered at a local shelter, serving meals to families who had fallen on hard times, their faces reflecting stories written with hardship yet ignited with hope. With every warm plate she served, she witnessed not merely the satisfaction of hunger being quelled but the laughter that spilled forth from shared memories, creating an atmosphere where burdens felt lighter. There, in that humble setting, her presence was met with gratitude and kindness that transcended her initial intent of helping others. With each passing day, the people she met transformed her understanding of what it meant to truly be alive with purpose. Encouraged by this realization, Mia embarked on spreading her newfound appreciation for generosity throughout her surroundings, embarking upon what she would later come to see as a beautiful experiment in connection.

She began initiating small acts of kindness, eager to observe how they would ripple outward, much like the early morning light spilling through the leaves as dawn broke. She baked muffins for her neighbour, slyly including a few extras in the basket to share with the children on the street corner selling lemonade. Each gesture celebrated the beauty of human connection, and she began to notice as her small offerings inspired others to give as well. Where there had been silence on the street, laughter now echoed as parents and children played together in the park. An elderly couple even began hosting evening bonfires, inviting neighbours to share stories and laughter amid the flickering flames. It dawned on Mia that these simple, generous acts ignited a warmth within those around her, creating a sense of belonging that transcended any material wealth she once thought mattered. The neighbourhood transformed from a series of isolated homes into a vibrant tapestry of interwoven lives, rich with shared experiences and growing relationships.

One evening, as the sun sank below the horizon, painting the sky in hues of purple and gold, Mia gathered with newfound friends around the firepit. Laughter danced around her, and she felt the warmth of connection in a way she had never experienced before. One by one, stories unfolded like flowers blooming in the twilight—the tale of a single mother finding strength in community support, a young artist discovering encouragement from those who believed in her dreams, and the poignant story of an elderly man who, once riddled with loneliness, discovered companionship through the generosity of his neighbours. Each story spoke of how a simple act, a kind word, or an open door transformed lives, illuminating her belief that generosity served as a binding agent for human experiences. Mia watched as these threads of connection deepened, intertwining the lives of everyone gathered until she could almost see the web glistening in the dusky light, a manifestation of love circulating through every heart present.

Mia soon became a tireless advocate for nurturing generosity, believing firmly that it held the power to create sanctuary-like spaces where people felt a sense of belonging. Inspired, she organized a neighbourhood gathering, encouraging everyone to share their skills. During this 'Community Day,' the clamour of laughter and wisdom filled the air as strangers became friends, each contribution enriching the community tapestry a little further. One resident demonstrated weaving techniques she had learned from her grandmother, crafting colourful mats out of discarded fabric, while another demonstrated gardening tricks that turned ordinary balconies into urban jungles. With every shared idea, resource, and ounce of encouragement exchanged, the community was woven a little tighter, each knot symbolizing an unbreakable bond formed through generosity.

As weeks turned into months, Mia marvelled at how her own life had transformed as a result of these generous acts. Invitations from neighbours began pouring in, reminding her that she was no longer just a solitary figure adrift but part of a collective heartbeat. She attended potlucks next door where culinary traditions mingled, each dish a narrative steeped in culture, history, and inexhaustible love. Conversations strayed into whimsical territories, with children's laughter ringing vibrant against the backdrop of family banter, underscoring the beauty passionately woven into the fabric of her community. As friendships blossomed, Mia felt the presence of that intangible warmth she had longed for, possessing an authenticity that no lavish home could provide. The richness of her life sprang forth not from what she possessed materialistically, but from the abundance she found in the connections she nurtured and the love she spread around her.

Ultimately, Mia's journey of generosity unravelled layers of understanding within her, revealing how giving was never a loss but, rather, a divine investment. Each act of kindness she bestowed sent appreciative ripples into the universe, creating pathways for love and compassion to return to her, often in profound and unexpected ways. There was a sense of divine orchestration at play, an interwoven dance of souls seeking connection, buoyed by a shared understanding of the simplicity of kindness. And so, along her path of discovery, Mia not only learned that a rich home was not defined by opulence but intricately crafted by intertwining lives supporting one another through generosity. Each ripple emerged not merely as a benevolent gesture but as a manifestation of God's grace, as nourishing as the earth, reminding her that love and home flourish most in the richness of community.

16

A HOMECOMING OF MEMORIES

As Mia approached the weathered gates of her childhood home, she felt the stirring of emotions that threatened to engulf her, an overwhelming tide of nostalgia and longing. The once-vibrant colours of the home had faded, much like the memories of her early years that had dulled with time—yet the essence of love and connection she had experienced within those walls remained vivid in her heart. With each hesitant step forward, the echoes of laughter, the warmth of familial bonds, and the scent of home-cooked meals wrapped around her like a familiar embrace. She remembered the way the sunlight poured through the windows, creating dancing patterns on the wooden floor, a canvas where her dreams had once been painted.

The garden was overgrown, a wild tangle of weeds that seemed to vie for attention, yet within that chaos, the fragrant blooms of jasmine and the cheerful dance of dandelions whispered the stories of her childhood. Here, she recalled the afternoons spent chasing fireflies, the gentle hands of her parents guiding her in the art of planting. Each seedling, each flower, was a testament to their love, nurtured over time, much like the family dynamics woven into her very being. As she wandered through the garden, tendrils of memories wrapped around her heart; she could almost hear the soft voices of her mother and father imbued with laughter and encouragement, their eyes sparkling like the stars they would watch together at night.

In her mind's eye, she could see her younger self, fearless and exuberant, leaping into her father's arms as he returned from work, the world melting away into that singular moment of joy. It was a reckless abandon that embodied the absolute trust a child places in the love of their parents. She could taste the sweetness of those long-lost summers where time was nothing but a playful breeze—fresh lemonade, water balloon fights, and bedtime stories curling up beneath the patchwork quilt her grandmother had stitched with care.

As Mia stepped into the dimly lit attic of her ancestral home, a cascade of dust danced in the sunbeams that filtered through the cracks of the old wooden beams above. Each moted glimmer caught her breath, momentarily mesmerizing her as she stood at the threshold of her family's history. The air was thick with a musty fragrance, the unmistakable scent of time gone by, an echo of stories waiting to be told. Just as the sunlight washed over her skin, she felt a wave of warmth wrap around her heart, as if the spirits of her ancestors were welcoming her back home. With each hesitant step forward, she brushed aside cobwebbed corners and stored away vestiges of a life that once thrived, seeking to unearth treasures hidden not only in the attic but also in the very fabric of her existence.

The first piece of family history she came across was an ornate wooden chest; its delicate carvings almost lost under layers of dust—a testament to someone's careful craftsmanship. Kneeling down, she took a deep breath before lifting the heavy lid. The sound of hinges creaking like an old poem fluttering through time filled the attic. Inside, she found a collection of worn letters, brittle and yellowed with age. They were tangled and tied together with a silk ribbon, their ink faded yet vibrant in her imagination. Mia gently unfolded one of the letters and began to read, the script transforming her surroundings. It was a love letter from her great-grandfather to her great-grandmother, filled with nostalgia and promises that transcended the barriers of time. His words embodied a longing that echoed through the decades, revealing a love fierce and unwavering, inherently grounded in trust and shared dreams. Each line was a brushstroke filling the canvas of her heart, awakening her to the notion that love was, and always would be, the cornerstone of their family legacy.

With a profound sense of connection, Mia placed the letter back into the chest and continued her exploration. As she sifted through the remnants, she uncovered a patchwork quilt, its colours muted by age yet vibrant in the stories they cradled. Each stitch imbued in the fabric told a tale of hardship and celebration, of family gatherings around fireside tales and soothing lullabies whispered to children. As the quilt unfolded before her, Mia found herself enveloped in warmth, not just from the physical attributes of the quilt, but from the very essence of the women who had sewn it together. She could almost hear the laughter of her grandmother, feel the loving touch of her mother as they nestled under its embrace. It was a tapestry stitched with love, symbolizing resilience against the harshness of the world outside, a reminder that a home is not merely a place, but a refuge crafted through collective love and enduring warmth.

Raiding further into the depths of the attic, Mia stumbled upon a delicate porcelain doll, its porcelain face untouched despite the years gone by. It was a relic from her childhood, a reflection of innocence, care, and cherished moments shared with her family. Bonding over stories that came alive in the presence of that doll, she could see her own reflection—the girl who had been too young to understand the weight of legacy, too innocent to grasp the importance of love that transcended generations. It was as if the doll had witnessed every laugh, every whispered secret, every tear shed in moments of joy and sorrow. In that moment of rediscovery, Mia felt an appreciation swell within her for the life lessons wrapped within the very fibres that constituted her family. Her ancestors had poured their hopes and dreams into this doll, crafting not just a toy but an emblem of care, of nurturing a lineage that would carry forward stories bound in affection.

As she navigated through the labyrinth of family artifacts, the narrative of her lineage began unfolding like an intricate tapestry. An array of photographs, sepia-toned and tinged with nostalgia, adorned the walls of her memory, creating a gallery of faces that mirrored her own. Each portrait told a story; histories etched on the faces of those who had journeyed before her. There was her grandfather with eyes shimmering with mischief, the smile on her great-aunt's face captured mid-laughter, the kindness that radiated from her great-grandmother's gentle gaze—it was a living tableau of love and heartbreak, of laughter blended with tears. In each image, she saw fragments of herself, reflections that reminded her that she belonged to something far greater, an enduring legacy rooted not in wealth or status, but in the strength of family bonds tempered by time.

It was in this confluence of past and present that the depth of her discovery dawned upon her. With every crumbling artifact, she unearthed not just memories but a trove of values that had shaped her identity. The ancestral threads woven into her being urged her to celebrate authenticity, to embrace the richness derived from relationships, and to recognize that true wealth lies in the beauty of connection. Sitting amid this vibrant history, Mia realized that her family's story was not confined to material possessions or constructed legacies; it was a living entity, alive in the stories shared, the sacrifices made, and the love that continually bridged generations. The dust of time did not merely cloak these artifacts; it was a testament to the resilience of love, the grit of community, and the warmth of shared experiences that had carved a home within her heart.

Later, as she stood in her old bedroom, surrounded by remnants of her innocence—the collection of fairy tales stacked high on the shelves, the scribbled notes of dreams and whispers of hopes tucked under her pillow—she felt a gentle tug at her heart to make space for the life lessons hidden within those belongings. The soft hues of her bedding still felt like a fortress against the uncertainties of the world outside, and in that haven, she remembered the countless nights she had spent recounting her day to her stuffed animals, pouring all her fears and joys into the fabric of her imagination, learning early on the power of vulnerability. It struck her profoundly that family ties were as much about the people we choose to surround ourselves with, as they were about those who were tied to us by lineage.

Mia recalled the day of her high school graduation, where the proud smiles of her loved ones illuminated the ceremony, each face turning toward her like flowers in search of sunlight. In that moment, she had felt buoyed by a mixture of love and pride, yet the pleasure was bittersweet; now, she understood the fleeting nature of time. Those smiles had not only conveyed joy but also carried the weight of their sacrifices and hopes for her future. She grasped how family was a sanctuary; it was a repository of affection where one could lay their burdens down and find solace in the acceptance of one another's flaws and dreams. As the sun dipped low in the sky, casting a golden glow around her, she cradled the idea that true wealth lies not in material possessions but in the warm tapestry of relationships nurtured with love—relationships that possess the capacity to weave together separate lives into a single shared narrative.

Amidst the echoes of memories, she found herself conjuring the stories that belonged to each corner of the house—the creaking boards of the hallway that she had once sprinted down, the warmth of her mother's kitchen bursting with laughter and the inviting aroma of her signature dishes wafting out to greet her as she arrived home from school. In those moments, Mia recognized the richness of her emotional lineage, the laughter that sparkled like sunshine, the tears that watered the roots of compassion, and the hugs that mended wounds invisible to the eye. In a world that often chased the allure of wealth and status, Mia understood now that these familial ties—the cheerful camaraderie of friends, the unwavering presence of her family—crafted the framework of a rich home.

With renewed vigour and a gentle smile tracing her lips, Mia vowed to cherish the enchantment woven into the fabric of her family ties, to celebrate the stories of affection that echoed through time, and to shape her life based on the genuine connections that fortified her spirit. She knew now that happiness was not the endpoint of a search for something greater or more bountiful. Rather, it was the journey taken with those who walked alongside her, a heartfelt adventure that formed the essence of what it meant to call a place home—rooted in love, nourished by trust, and adorned with the warm embrace of shared experiences that brought light to even the darkest of days. In this realization, she discovered the transformative power of rich, emotional legacy—the inheritance far greater than any material wealth could ever bestow.

Motivated to breathe new life into the house, Mia called upon her friends and the community that had embraced her journey with open arms. It was during this gathering that she felt the true power of togetherness, a force that ignited the beginnings of renewal. Together, they stripped away years of dust and despair, unearthing forgotten treasures buried beneath layers of neglect. The physical labour was infused with laughter, stories, and shared hopes, each scraped wall and hoisted beam strengthening the bonds of connection. As they painted walls in warm hues inspired by the sunsets he loved, Mia could feel her ancestors smiling down upon them, their presence woven into the very fabric of the space they were revitalizing.

Yet it wasn't merely the act of renewal that proved transformative for Mia; it was within the enclosed conversations shared over cups of steaming tea in rooms that once echoed sorrow. During those moments, the elephant in the room—the anxieties and loneliness that often plagued her—was carefully unpacked, allowing each of her friends to share their own stories of longing and the universal search for home. The walls absorbed their hopes and dreams, loudly declaring their commitment to filling the space with kindness and compassion. There, among the creaking floorboards and sun-drenched windows, Mia basked in a newly forged sense of purpose, realizing that it wasn't just the physical space being rebuilt but the very foundation of intimate relationships that were being forged anew.

Soon, Mia's vision doubled down, shifting from merely a renovation project into a pilgrimage—a sacred quest to honour her family's past while paving the way for a vibrantly rich future. She ventured back into the community she had often overlooked in her search for something grand, grasping the hands of those who dedicated their lives to crafting relationships dense with loyalty and friendship. The monk she had encountered in her travels imparted profound wisdom during a community gathering, noting that what we often seek in material wealth can always be found in the hearts of those we cherish. It pushed her to engage even deeper with her own heart, provoking a profound reckoning with her own fears of inadequacy that had previously clouded her judgment. It taught her to see her family home not just as a physical structure but as a microcosm of all those pivotal relationships that completed her life.

Mia learned the beauty of embracing imperfection as she filled the house with mementos—not with the intent to showcase extravagance but to reflect the character and history that imbued every corner. She hung photographs that framed not just faces but moments: her mother laughing amidst friends, her father giggling with siblings, a long-lost cousin attempting a culinary disaster. Each carefully placed item blended with fresh flowers from the local market, echoing messages of renewal, serenity, and vitality. With every thud of the hammer and every stroke of the brush, Mia was transforming not just a house but the very narrative of what it meant to call a place 'home.'

It was during a quiet moment, after the final coat of paint was completed, that she truly felt it—a resonant buzz that felt like the heartbeat of the house returning. This was more than bricks fitted together; it was a sanctuary constructed of love transformed and revived. Here, within these walls, the legacies of both her ancestors and her own journey clasped hands, bridging the past with the present and melding the two into something spectacularly alive. Mia sank into the comforting embrace of a well-worn armchair, cocooned in the warmth of her friends mingling, vibrating with laughter and joy.

Mia recognized her family legacy—an inheritance of resilience, adaptability, and love—was no longer something stored in fragmented memories but rather alive, breathing, and pulsing within the very core of this home. In reclaiming it, she had also reclaimed herself; it became evident that true richness was not merely a possession but a mosaic of experiences, community connections, and above all, love. The house was not just a backdrop for life, but a central character woven into the fabric of her existence that would facilitate relationships that nourished her soul.

As twilight descended, Mia joined her friends outside to witness the stars twinkling against the velvety night sky. Each shimmering light twinkled like the laughter that echoed within the walls, a chorus celebrating the confluence of past and present. The profound realization washed over her: within that space, they had woven a tapestry of love unparalleled, and now, together, they could navigate the future, creating new memories to adorn the halls—memories that would flow through her family home like an everlasting ember, ensuring that its flame would never again die.

As if summoned by her return, members of her family began to trickle in, drawn like moths to a flame. Uncles and aunts, cousins and siblings—all arriving with stories to share and laughter to rekindle. Each embrace felt like a soft reminder of the wealth they all carried within their hearts; she basked in the wealth of connection they shared, and for the first time in years, Mia felt the weight of loneliness lift, transformed into something lighter and far more enduring. They gathered together on the front porch, the evening air spiced with the sweetness of memories and the promise of new beginnings. The rhythmic creak of the old rocking chairs harmonized with the chorus of familial laughter as old tales spilled forth, weaving together the fabric of their shared experience in a comforting quilt that wrapped around them. The stories flowed effortlessly, not just words, but the essence of who they were, laced with the richness of their experience, illuminating the roles of each family member like the warm glow of lanterns at dusk.

Mia absorbed every word as fruity laughter danced between them, painting vivid scenes that brought the past to life—all those simple moments that held profound meaning. Her heart swelled with appreciation, recognizing now that these connections were the true wealth of their lineage. As they spoke, each tale was punctuated with the remnants of shared meals, snippets of music played, and poems recited in candlelit rooms. Amidst the exchange of these cherished narratives, Mia realized that every one of these moments contributed to the legacy she yearned to embrace. The mundane had transformed into the extraordinary, the simplicity of family life morphing into a magnificent tapestry that conveyed profound love—elements that had shaped her identity.

Mia felt the glue of their shared memories forge new dimensions within her heart, pulling together the strands of camaraderie that were often overlooked in the rush of life. Sparked by conviviality, they decided to cook in the age-old kitchen, where time seemed to stand still, and the spirit of their ancestors guided them. They chopped and stirred, singing anthems of laughter, demonstrating how embracing each present moment filled their hearts with abundance. The smells of spices mingled with the sound of nostalgic tunes, reawakening the spirit of family gatherings from long ago. Through the clattering of pots and the warmth of shared laughter, they painted not just a meal but a feast celebrating their lineage, a meal that transcended conventional cooking, morphing into a rite woven with love and purpose.

As they gathered around the table, Mia looked around at the faces she cherished, illuminated by flickering candlelight, and understood that this was the fabled richness she had been seeking. The clinks of glasses promised joy as they toasted to the bonds that held them together, to the essence of trust that was the foundation of their family. In that moment, Mia understood the immeasurable value of these connections—generations intertwined by love, hardship, resilience, laughter, and sorrow. Each face reflected shared struggles and triumphs—the lessons learned and passed down like sacred relics shared across time.

With every bite they savoured and every laughter they shared, her family was not merely filling their bellies but also nourishing the very soul of their lineage. Mia felt a swell of gratitude, an overwhelming sense of purpose rising within her, propelling her toward the call of her ancestors—the mission to ensure that their incredible stories and lessons were not lost to the winds of time. Each heart-to-heart exchange became a touchpoint that anchored her to this rich heritage, forming an invisible thread that reached out like roots from an ancient tree, grounding her while allowing her to grow upward toward the sky.

As the evening wore on and the stars began to peek shyly through the velvety darkness, it became apparent to Mia that this gathering was not just a reunion; it was a revival of spirit, the rekindling of what it meant to have a rich home—not built of bricks and mortar, but of trust, respect, love, and shared history. Here, illuminated by the soft glow between them, she realized that the house she had once seen as forsaken was thriving in its essence, pulsating with the vibrancy of living memories. And so, a vision unfolded in her heart: her calling to reestablish this home—not merely as a dwelling but as a living entity nourishing every soul that crossed its threshold, creating a sacred space for laughter, learning, sharing, and loving.

As they celebrated, Mia sat back and absorbed their lively conversations, her heart swelling with visions of family gatherings yet to come, joyful reunions solidifying their traditions, perpetuating this rich legacy for generations yet unborn. A profound understanding ignited within her—home was indeed a collection of these transient moments, intrinsic to hearts beating in sync with one another. True wealth lies in the connections made in shared experiences, echoing through the very fabric of humanity. And so, in this gathering of the heart, Mia found the purpose of her quest—a rich home no longer parallel to the world's worldly treasures but as a beacon of love and resilience resting in the sacredness of each other. With newfound resolve, she embraced her family around her—an interconnected web of love, healing, and selfless empathy—and together, they solidified a legacy that would resonate through the ages, rekindled by the enduring spirit of their past, igniting the flames of hope in their future.

17

THE HEALING PROCESS

In the stillness of the early morning, when the air carried a crispness that whispered secrets of the rising sun, Mia found herself wandering through the overgrown garden of her ancestral home. The earth beneath her feet was damp with dew, glistening like scattered diamonds, and as she inhaled deeply, the heady fragrances of blooming wildflowers intertwined with earthy soil filled her senses. It was a garden once tended to with love—an extension of the family's essence, now faintly echoing memories of laughter, warmth, and familial bonds that had weathered the seasons of life. As she ambled along the path, each step seemed to unlock a myriad of emotions, deep-rooted and intertwined with the very fabric of her being. As she stood amidst the blooming chaos of her heritage, she recognized that true freedom lay right there, nestled in the fertile soil of her heart—waiting patiently for her to excavate it.

In the quiet moments spent in counsels with the wise monk, a flicker of understanding ignited within her. He had often spoken of forgiveness as an act of self-liberation, a personal alchemy that transformed the bitter roots of resentment into blooms of compassion. "Forgiveness is not about absolving others; it is about freeing ourselves," he had gently stated. That truth resonated with her, transforming the concept from a burden to bear into an offering of grace—a salve for her own wounds. Gazing at the wildflowers swaying in the gentle breeze, Mia began to connect the dots in her heart; each little flower represented a moment of her familial strife, a grievance stuffed away like forgotten debris in the attic of her memory. She envisioned herself gently brushing away the dust, giving light to long-neglected corners, and in doing so, she became more than just a bystander in her own narrative—she became the curator of her legacy.

Taking the lessons from the monk, Mia began to explore the intricacies of her family's history, seeking the stories behind the actions that had once caused her so much hurt. It became clear that each family member had embarked on their unique journeys, often battling their own demons and pasts. Her father, swathed in stoicism, was not just a figure of authority but a man who confronted loss through distance, guarding his heart with walls built high. Her mother, forever smiling, bore the weight of sacrifice—a silent warrior who had handed her heart over to the family at the expense of her own needs. They were flawed, intricate beings with their unique histories—interwoven threads in the elaborate tapestry of her existence. Recognizing this complexity was a foundation upon which Mia started reconstructing the bridges that had begun to crumble, viewing her family through a lens softened by understanding rather than edged with bitterness.

As she dug deeper, she began to see the beauty nestled in imperfection, reminiscent of the artisan who moulded clay—not a perfect symmetry but rather a tribute to the rawness of the earth. Each encounter with her father and mother turned from encounters steeped in tension to conversations drenched in vulnerability. Sitting beside her mother on a sunlit porch, they shared not just words but emotions, unravelling the knots that bound them to isolation. Mia witnessed tears tracing paths down her mother's cheeks—a testament to years of masked feelings and unexpressed needs flooding into the open. In that exchange, forgiveness was no longer a monologue but a dialogue—a sharing of truths in a space filled with silence, inviting both to release the heavy burdens they had inadvertently placed upon one another.

Just as the wise monk had taught her, Mia learned that forgiveness must flow from deep understanding. As memories resurfaced, she endeavoured to validate her parents' feelings while also graciously addressing her own. She understood that to let go of her hurt, she must allow herself to engage with their stories, blending threads of her pain with their experiences and creating a narrative ripe for healing. In the evenings spent sharing meals around the dining table, which had long taken on a dust-covered aesthetic as both a reminder and a grieving post, laughter sometimes erupted, punctuated by the sweetness of nostalgia. They shared tales of old family adventures, new insights revealed through the lens of their experiences, allowing them to shift out from shadows into light, learning to appreciate the laughter rather than just focusing on the strife.

Forgiveness became a gentle tide that swept through their conversations, allowing them to reclaim lost time and leverage shared understanding. Mending the cracks in their relationships proved to be an exploration rather than a destination. They stumbled at times, sometimes falling back into misunderstandings or stubborn silences, but Mia slowly recognized that each misstep was not a failure but an integral part of the healing process. Her heart opened in ways she had only envisioned in dreams, each day painting a fresh canvas—a beautiful assemblage of colours both bright and muted, depicting their family not as broken, but as on a journey towards wholeness.

Simultaneously, she understood that the journey of forgiveness extended beyond her immediate family; it beckoned her to release any lingering grudges that coloured her past relationships within the community that surrounded her. It prompted Mia to revisit connections she had allowed to wither away under the weight of resentment, rekindling friendships by extending understanding and compassion that she had discovered within herself. She sought out acquaintances with whom she had experienced discord, embarking on a pilgrimage to humble herself, to initiate dialogues that felt long overdue. Each conversation was a release—a healing balm on the ones who had strayed, allowing her to let go of the burdens that had weighed down her spirit. The connections came alive again—new roots swirling and intertwining in the soil of forgiveness, flourishing into vibrant relationships founded not just on healing but also on authenticity.

Mia's journey was punctuated by moments that felt pivotal, each revealing the profound depth of the human experience—teaching her that to embrace forgiveness in its entirety meant to relish in the vulnerability of relationships. It was in her vulnerability that she found connection; from bare emotions deepened friendships sprouted. The more she engaged with the world around her, the more light was drawn into her own sanctuary—her heart transforming into a garden teeming with love, overflowing with acceptance. It became a rich tapestry woven from understanding, threading peace and joy into the lives of those who walked beside her—turning each moment into a celebration of the human spirit.

This was the moment she had been waiting for, a moment steeped in courage as she committed herself to reach out to her parents. Gripping her phone tightly, she let her breath be the anchor to calm her racing thoughts. The act of sending a simple message felt monumental—but she knew that vulnerability was what would set her free. "Can we talk? I'm home." The words hovered before her fingers, as she dared to press 'send', a pivotal move toward healing the rift that had grown between them. Mia took a step back, watching as the blue circle of the message indicator spun. In that instant, she recognized that this act of connection was a powerful testament to her growth and the embodiment of her commitment to embrace a flourishing future filled with love, trust, and understanding.

The waiting felt infinite, each passing second a reminder of the tension that had woven itself into the fabric of her family life. Yet Mia had made a choice; her heart now pulsed with a fervent belief in the power of forgiveness, knowing that it had the potential to dismantle the barriers that pain had constructed. As each breath steadied her resolve, a small vibration in her pocket startled her. She glanced at the screen, where her mother's name glowed brightly, her heart leaping as she hurriedly opened the message. "I'd like that, sweetheart. I've missed you." The words were simple yet heavy with meaning, a thread extending between them that promised connection and healing. Tears welled in her eyes as she felt the weight of emotional baggage lift, realizing that forgiveness was the key to stepping into a future suffused with the richness of familial love, a foundation upon which true homes are built.

Moments later, Mia found herself face-to-face with her parents in the living room, the same space that had witnessed so many important milestones of their lives together. The room had dimmed, lit only by the soft glow of a lamp perched on the side table, creating a cocoon-like atmosphere that felt safe, despite the vulnerability that lay ahead. Her mother's eyes shimmered with glistening emotions, while her father's expression bore the weight of apprehension and hope intermingled. The walls seemed to echo their unspoken feelings, brimming with years of silence that begged for release. As Mia gathered the courage to speak, she felt a lightness envelop her, a fortifying warmth she had so desperately sought—this was the moment of re-connection, an opportunity to share not just her heart, but also to listen deeply and understand theirs.

"I'm sorry for the distance," Mia began, her voice wavering slightly, "for the walls I built between us. It was never about you, but my own confusion and hurt. I've realized that our family is worth fighting for." The words spilled forth, a garland of honesty wrapped in a promise to be better, to be more present and engaged. Her mother's brow furrowed, as she struggled to hold back her tears. The unseasoned anger, she now knew, had stemmed from fear—fear of losing her daughter to the tides of life. As Mia's heartfelt admission settled in the room, she saw her parents visibly soften, the tension thawing in the wake of vulnerability exposed.

The conversation flowed like a gentle stream, filled with careful words and shared stories, a weaving of their experiences that had brought them to this pivotal moment. Mia listened attentively, absorbing the burdens her parents had carried alone, laden with the guilt and sadness of misunderstanding one another. It was as though, together, they were untangling a ball of yarn, slowly unravelling the knots that had formed over the years. With each revelation shared, they chipped away at the barriers that had separated them, piecing together the fragments of hurt and ultimately sharing the joy of rediscovering one another.

In that sanctuary of their home, laughter permeated the air as they recounted cherished memories, the joyous milestones that had celebrated their togetherness, echoing the simple pleasures of life that had once felt lost. Mia felt the palpable shift in the atmosphere—the shadows of the past were beginning to dissolve, transformed by the warmth of connection that reignited hope. Here was the richness of their heritage, the love that had forged their lives. She grasped the significance of these moments, realizing that they carved an indelible path toward a harmonious future. Forgiveness offered not just solace, but a fertile ground for love—the very foundation of the rich home she had so ardently sought.

And so, amid the tears and laughter, Mia could see that embracing her future meant embracing vulnerability, for it was the frailty of those moments that laid bare the strength of their bonds. With renewed gratitude, she acknowledged the lessons of her journey—the wise teachings of the Elder had echoed in her mind as she navigated through forgiveness and connection. That radiant light of love infusing the very essence of their house felt like an embrace of the Divine, a gentle reminder that grace and redemption are found even amidst our deepest struggles.

As the night deepened, Mia grasped her parents' hands within her own, intertwining their fingers, creating a circle of unity that felt both sacred and divine. More than mere family, they were a tapestry woven with threads of love, trust, and mutual commitment to one another. With the dawn of tomorrow, new memories would arise, radiant and teeming with the possibilities that forgiveness had unveiled—a rich home was not just a place; it blossomed from the courage to forgive and love, and that was the legacy that Mia vowed to maintain. Amid life's unpredictable ebbs and flows, the strength of their family bond would illuminate the paths ahead, guiding them to embrace the future with hearts wide open and ready to forge deeper connections, prompting their home to flourish in the richness of love and enduring togetherness.

Through these challenges, Mia learned that a welcoming spirit required not only the joy of exchange but also a commitment to understanding one another. As her community navigated conflicts and emerged in newfound solidarity, she was struck by the truth that with every crack that appeared in their collective armour, they forged deeper connections, revealing the tender humanity lurking beneath. Each resolution became a celebration of growth, a testament to their commitment to one another and their shared vision of a rich home—one where conversations could flow freely, and healing could take root.

With time, Mia's ancestral home became a luminous symbol of the warmth and community spirit that enveloped them. As the echoes of laughter wove through the air, transforming an ordinary house into something extraordinary, she held onto the belief that her vision had sparked something profound—a movement toward love and trust that radiated outward, inviting more hearts into the fold. Her welcoming spirit set the stage for a microcosm of life filled with rich experiences, where everything from shared meals to spontaneous late-night conversations added texture to the canvas of their community.

The beauty of a rich home evolved beyond bricks and walls; it thrived in the authenticity of every moment shared and every story told. True richness began to emerge from the collective heartbeat of the community, an unseen force that connected them all. Mia stood and watched as her once forlorn ancestral home burgeoned into a lively centre of life, reflecting the love and trust invested in it, confirming what she had always believed: that a welcoming spirit, rooted in authenticity and grace, can indeed create a home—the kind that is not forged through material wealth, but through the genuine connections that bless her life and others alike.

During winter's chill, when nights became longer and shadows danced in the corners of the house, Mia and her friends devised a series of seasonal gatherings, blending warmth and connection through various festivities. They celebrated the winter solstice with light and laughter, adorning the house with handmade decorations that represented their communal experiences. Candles glimmered in the windows like beacons of hope and connection drawing others home. As the resonance of their shared spirits filled the air, she realized they were crafting not merely a seasonal tradition but a legacy of togetherness that would continue long after their individual stories had shifted into the pages of life. She envisioned future generations hosting their gatherings, continuing to weave the threads of community that they had so deliberately intertwined. Each event served not just to celebrate the warmth of friendship but to cultivate gratitude for the diverse gifts offered by each individual, no matter how small, reaffirming the beauty of human connection.

Through her relentless dedication, the house emerged as a vibrant emblem of the love-rich sanctuary she had long envisioned. In what had once felt like a mere echo of a forgotten past, she now witnessed life flourishing through the laughter of children playing, the stories of elders being celebrated, and the warmth of those who gathered to create a transformative spirit. Her quest for a rich home—one utterly paid for not in currency but in grace, connection, and unconditional love—had come full circle. The essence of a home long illuminated by the love and laughter of those who remembered its heart now thrived in the gentle embrace of community bonds. And in this transformation, amid the laughter and the chatter, the memories of those who had passed whispering through the walls, Mia ultimately discovered that home is not a destination but a continuous journey enriched with every person who walks through its door, lending pieces of their spirit to the very heart that welcomes them.

Mia began to speak, her voice warm as honey, drawing the attention of the crowd as she welcomed them to this feast of love. She shared how this home, once echoing with an emptiness she had felt so deeply, was now bursting with life, colour, and laughter. This transformation was the result of all gathered here, the product of love caught in the web of lives intertwining, growing, enriching one another. She felt a tear slip down her cheek, reflecting both joy and a deep remembrance of all that had been lost and found.

With the acknowledgment of their shared journey, Mia invited each person to share their stories, and as words flowed, the air thickened with emotion. The Elder, with his eyes twinkling like bright coals in the crackling fire, recounted tales of resilience and trust, of loving without boundaries and how these bonds had cultivated a community that felt more like family. The Monk, embodying a serenity that enveloped all around him, spoke gently about spiritual nourishment, reflecting on how the simplest aspects of life could create a sanctuary filled with peace. As every story was shared, Mia felt the fabric of their collective experience expand, invite, and settle into a comforting embrace, weaving through the layers of their hearts, creating connections that promised to linger long after the night faded into memory.

Laughter erupted as stories stirred echoes and memories tangled with threads of humour—tales of misadventures at local fairs, of baking mishaps that resulted in unexpected favours, and of moments where love shone brightly even in the mundane. It was a banquet embellished with all the ingredients that made up the essence of life: joy, struggle, celebration, and the unity that emerged from overcoming obstacles together.

As the evening descended deeper into night, Mia arranged a small token of love—a simple piece of clay moulded into a heart—crafted by the Artisan earlier that day. She presented this keepsake as a reminder that every person, with their uniqueness, contributed to the filling of her heart, enriching her existence through their love and togetherness. It was a physical representation of the feast they now shared, a bond forged through stories, laughter, and an unwavering commitment to one another.

The culmination of the evening saw songs being sung, voices rising to blend harmoniously like a beautiful tapestry woven from laughter and shared dreams. The melodies that lingered in the warm air stirred angelic echoes throughout the night. Each person waved their voices in tribute to the beauty of the moment, the gift of togetherness that cocooned them like the very stars that twinkled overhead. The richness they had discovered within one another during their journey resonated in this place—they witnessed the transformative power of love, the kind that wrapped around you and whispered that no matter their differences, they could rise together, bound by the sentiments they held dear.

As the feast wound to a close, cheeks flushed with warmth, hands filled with empty plates, and bellies full of flavours that danced on their tongues, Mia silently reflected on the magic of it all. The celebration had illuminated her heart to the truth she'd come to understand on this journey: a wealthy home was not calculated in terms of bricks, mortar, or material wealth but in the immeasurable value of love that flowed abundantly. It thrived in the moments they shared, the laughter that echoed from corner to corner, the tears shed in joy and sorrow alike.

The final gathering was a circle—a sacred embrace that bundled them together in unity. Underneath the twinkling stars, they joined hands, forming a living testament to the strength of their interconnectedness. As they shared their wishes for one another, Mia felt enveloped in grace, resonating with an overwhelming sense of belonging that left her heart brimming with joy.

As the night painted its final strokes, the friends and family began to disperse into the shadows of twilight, their spirits entwined and hearts enriched. In that moment, surrounded by love, connection, and the comforting embrace of community, Mia understood that she had indeed found her rich home—a haven built not with money but with the laughter, warmth, and genuine bonds that transcended the material world.

Mia knew that while paths may diverge, love would reunite them. A comforting sense of belonging would persist, grounded in shared experiences and the threads of connection they had woven together. She imagined a family board adorned with colourful sticky notes of events to plan, highlighting milestones, festivities, and even moments meant for quiet reflection—the juxtaposition of celebration and contemplation creating a delicate balance that would feed their souls. Life itself, in all its multifaceted forms, would be acknowledged and cherished, and the home would stand as a testament to the power of community, where everyone found refuge, warmth, and the understanding that home is built in the hearts of those who fill it with love.

18

PASSING DOWN THE WISDOM

The laughter of children echoed through the halls, a delightful choir that resonated with the very essence of what it meant to be home. This place, once abandoned, now pulsed with life, transformed by the love, trust, and community she had woven into its very fabric. In the heart of this revival lay a deep-seated desire to share the invaluable lessons she had learned, to pass down the wisdom that had blossomed within her like the resilient blooms in the garden outside. The journey she undertook to awaken her body and spirit also provided fertile ground for the minds of the next generation, those young souls eager to discover not just the bricks and mortar of a house but the intangible riches that made it a sanctuary.

Gathered around the wooden table that had been polished to a soft sheen from generations of hands patting its surface, Mia's family and friends formed a circle of radiant smiles, faces brimming with curiosity. As she stared into the eyes of her young nephew, Aadi, she felt the weight of responsibility settle upon her. It was as though the walls themselves breathed a sigh of expectation, urging her to ignite within them a flame of understanding, a yearning for the deeper connections that would sustain them throughout their lives. "I want to tell you a story," she began, her voice steady and inviting, "one that weaves through time, through the laughter and tears, the challenges and triumphs that we all face." As the children settled in, their grips on their little chairs tightened in anticipation, Mia transported them to her own childhood, a time when the allure of material possessions seemed all-consuming, a backdrop painted in vibrant colours yet lacking the substance she now cherished.

In her narrative, she recounted her earliest memories of the family home, steeped in nostalgia, when every creak of the floorboards and sway of the window blinds felt like an embrace. She spoke of the lavish parties that once filled the halls with unwanted hollow laughter, serving as a facade for the loneliness that crept in around the corners of her youth. It was a vivid recollection—faces adorned with perfectly crafted smiles, the sound of clinking glasses, and the fleeting allure of opulence that dissipated like smoke with the morning sun. As Aadi's eyes widened with wonder, Mia saw his reflection; he embodied an innocence that sought understanding, and she wished to safeguard that clarity from the blinding light of materialism. Her journey had taught her that true abundance unfurled from the connections forged through love and trust, something far richer than dollar signs could ever convey.

"But the most important part of this home," Mia continued, a soft smile playing on her lips, "is not the grand entrance or the perfectly manicured gardens; it’s the love that binds us together." Drawing into her message the tales of the figures who shaped her own journey—the wise artisan whose hands sculpted beauty from the simplest clay, the elder who poured wisdom into her heart with every shared cup of tea, and the tranquil monk whose meditative presence opened her eyes to the depths of her spirit—she painted vivid portraits of their roles in her life. Through their profound teachings, she emphasized that each act of kindness, each fleeting moment of honesty, and every gesture of togetherness was a thread woven into the tapestry that defined a family, binding them together in intricate designs of understanding.

As the sunlight slipped below the horizon, casting a soft twilight glow through the window, Mia's listeners leaned in as though they were drawn beyond the physicality of the room, transported to each scenario as they explored the landscapes of emotional wealth. "Love is the foundation," she insisted, her heart racing with every word. "It isn't always loud or flashy; sometimes it whispers. It manifests in the mundane moments: snuggling on a chilly evening, sharing meals that nourish not just the body, but the soul, or the comforting presence of someone who simply listens, without a need for words." She could see the spark of comprehension growing in their eyes, the realization that these moments carried the weight of meaning far beyond any physical gift.

She encouraged Aadi and the other children to cultivate their spaces with generosity, making room for others, be it a family member in need or a new friend at school. "Imagine a world where we could all offer kindness as freely as the sun offers warmth," she mused, her voice trembling with emotion. "It is in giving that we receive the greatest gifts, not only in friendships but in the sense of belonging it nurtures." With each pulse of her heart, she urged them to honour both their relationships and the lessons gleaned from shared experiences, framing them as treasures more profound than any expansive estate.

Mia felt a shift in the room, an electric vibe rippling as she spoke of honesty and authenticity—the indispensable ingredients for the relationship that she had cultivated over the years. She recounted the times she had faltered, the moments when fear held her tongue captive, and how it took monumental courage to stand firm in her truth. "Your path may ripple with challenges," she cautioned gently, "but being honest helps keep the colours of your relationships vibrant." The children nodded, fully attuned to the wisdom resonating from her voice. They understood that by sharing their truths; by embracing transparency, they could forge connections that were fortified against the inevitable storms life would throw their way.

Watering the seeds of generosity, Mia encouraged them to reflect on their intimate circles, inspiring thoughts about nurturing friendships beyond themselves. "Togetherness can transform us," she whispered, her voice now a lullaby. "When we support one another, share in each other's joys, and shoulder each other's burdens, we create a rich tapestry that weaves us into a community." She felt the warmth envelop her as the children murmured in agreement, their eyes bright with visions of unbreakable bonds blooming amid the love and compassion that emanated from her words.

As the evening light waned and shadows began to dance around them, Mia shared the beauty she discovered in every corner of her home, finding richness in the smallest details: the familiar comfort of a favourite blanket, the laughter shared over messy kitchen experiments, the love notes tucked between the pages of her old books, and even the bittersweet memories of loss that only served to deepen her appreciation for the present. "A rich home is not defined by what we possess, but by what we give, by the laughter echoing in our hallways and the warmth of shared memories that huddle together in our hearts," she said. The children were rapt with attention, unaware of time as it slipped away, held captive by the world Mia spun around them.

Bringing the night to a close, Mia spoke of her deep-seated affection for their family home, revealing how it was more than just a building filled with bricks and history; it was a living entity filled with memories that beckoned to be revived. "This place has cradled hurt, joy, struggles, and triumphs—it has seen all the threads that formed who I am," Mia reflected, her voice heavy with pride and gratitude. "That is why I pledge to keep it alive." She imparted this promise to her family, sharing her newfound mission to pass down this lineage of love, to preserve the essence of the home built upon trust and community while tending to the emotional landscape that lay within.

As the last rays of sunlight flickered, casting soft shadows across the room, the awe in the young faces surrounding her told her she had crafted a memory of their own—one they would carry with them as they grew, transforming their perceptions of home into something immeasurably rich. The stories Mia relayed weren't just her own; they resonated deeply with the hopes and dreams of every child present, igniting within them a new understanding of their legacy and the role they would play in nurturing the bonds of love that redefined what it meant to be home.

Mia felt fulfilled, as if a river of joy flowed through her, connecting her to each little heart, pulsing to the rhythm of trust, warmth, and belief in something greater than any one individual. The conversations they'd have in the years to come, the laughter shared during holidays, the tears in moments of loss—these would become the lifeblood of the family, enriching the walls of their home with voices woven into the fabric of eternity. As her family mulled over her stories, she vowed silently to keep sharing this wisdom, confronting each new generation with the challenge to unlock the hidden treasures that lay not in wealth but in their relationships.

Closing her eyes for a moment, Mia allowed herself to feel the embrace of their love enveloping her like a blanket, grounding her, reminding her of her purpose in carrying forth this legacy. The evening was no mere end; it was that shimmering golden dawn of a new beginning, one where she would continue to weave life into the walls of their home, ensuring that the richness intrinsic in their bonds would guide her family like stars illuminating the night sky. She had discovered that true wealth was borne of the heart, and in sharing this with the next generation, a cycle of hope and love continued, one that would reverberate through the lives of all who dared to see beyond the confines of material barriers, reaching toward the divine essence of what it truly meant to be home.

19

THE ENDLESS JOURNEY

As Mia stood at the threshold of her newly revitalized ancestral home, a gentle breeze wrapped around her like the comforting embrace of an old friend, whispering sweet nothings about the beauty of new beginnings. The walls of the house, once draped in languid despair, now radiated a warmth that felt like a hearth on a cold winter evening, glowing with the essence of love and connection. The vibrant flowers that adorned the garden danced rhythmically to nature's quiet symphony, and within each petal lay a promise—a promise that her journey was far from over. In that moment, Mia understood that what lies ahead was more than just a chapter in her life; it was an endless journey, a perpetual odyssey through the very fabric of existence itself, one that beckoned her to explore the depths of love, trust, and community.

In her pursuit of a rich home, encapsulated by bricks and mortar only in the loosest sense, Mia realized that home was not merely a destination but rather an evolving landscape, moulded by experience and nurtured through relationships. Each individual she met along the way—a wise monk perched upon a mountain peak offering sage advice, an elderly artisan kneading clay into breathtaking sculptures, or even the laughter of children echoing from the heart of the neighbourhood—became integral threads in the tapestry of her story. These encounters enriched her understanding of what it means to cultivate spaces where hearts beholding trust, honesty, and warmth could coexist and flourish. The endless journey was not merely her own, but a collective expedition shared with those who walked beside her, each stride echoing with the weight of countless stories intertwined in a beautiful, chaotic dance of connection.

Mia smiled at the vibrant community that had sprung up around her. Together they shared meals filled with laughter that resonated like music, homes punctuated by open doors, not just to enter but also to welcome the heart into a sanctuary of unconditional love. Here, the warmth of each gathered moment forged bonds stronger than steel, and it became evident that life on this journey meant extending compassion to others, inviting them to lay aside the masks worn in the glare of an unforgiving world. The lessons learned in humility and vulnerability sanctified the once empty space that now shimmered with laughter, trust, and an unconditional generosity that shaped a deeper connection to the self and to one another.

Driven by an insatiable curiosity, Mia began to explore the significance of nurturing relationships further, mindful that areas of her life deserved the same attention she bestowed on her home. She started volunteering at local shelters, offering a helping hand wrapped in empathy and understanding, transforming each encounter into an opportunity for learning and connection, finding fulfilment in the shared stories of struggle and resilience. Slivers of joy emerged from every act of kindness, and with each passing day, she became more aware that love ripples outward, each action a pendulum swinging through space and time, ultimately returning back to the giver with magnified intensity. She embraced the idea that generosity was not merely a gift of tangible things but one stemming from the heart, a force of nature that engulfed both giver and receiver in soothing warmth and profound grace.

In her quest, Mia also discovered the importance of creating a sanctuary conducive to personal growth and reflection. Moments spent by the fireplace unfolded like gentle whispers in her heart, urging her to nurture her own spirit amid the hustle and bustle of life. As soulful melodies graced her evenings, she infused the space with her dreams, aspirations, and a sense of serenity. It became a cocoon where she could shed the layers shaped by insecurity and self-doubt, revealing the beauty of authenticity. She understood that the enduring journey necessitated a commitment to herself, an investment rooted in self-love and acceptance. It allowed her to flourish, radiating with a newfound glow that beckoned others to bask in the gentle radiance of hope and fulfilment.

Mia also recognized that the very core of community lies in collective experiences—the shared laughter, the tears, the milestones, and the quiet moments woven between chaos and calmness. Each gathering with friends transformed into an opportunity for storytelling, their words sparking vivid imagery in the minds of both young and old while cementing the unyielding bonds of togetherness. They nurtured one another through life's seasons, celebrating victories big and small, providing pillow talk on sleepless nights, and collectively bearing the weight of heartache. Love thrived not just in joyful celebrations but also in moments of anguish where vulnerability became the cradle for shared recovery. The sanctuary she created flourished into a haven where both past wounds and present triumphs converged, each thread meticulously woven into the logbook of their intertwined lives.

With the passing seasons, Mia's home became a living testament to the journey she had undertaken. It was a canvas painted with brushstrokes of laughter that resonated through every hallway, a rich symphony reflecting the soul transformation that unfolded within its walls. In quiet evenings spent on her porch, surrounded by dear friends, they exchanged tender thoughts that flew like doves toward the sky—dispatches from the heart reminding them of how the pursuit of a rich home was ultimately about cherishing the fleeting moments that strung together the fabric of life itself. They understood that this infinite journey, filled with rich experiences and connections, served not only as a foundation for love but as an echo in the broader community. With each shared day, they began forging a legacy rooted in nurture, a promise passed down to future generations, solidly anchored in the belief that a home thrives in the collective hearts and hands that shape it.

In her heart, Mia carried a knowing that could not be assuaged; the endless journey would require her to continuously nurture and cultivate the richness of her home, for it would never become stagnant. She embraced the reality that life is a relentless teacher, with new lessons waiting to unfold the moment she opened herself to the world. As a lifelong student of love, trust, and community, she welcomed change while remaining rooted in the core values that had become the guiding star illuminating her path. Every sunrise presented an opportunity to connect more deeply and authentically with those around her, and the love she had gathered transformed into an ever-growing reservoir, offering sustenance to uplift and enrich not just her own life but also those of others. This interconnected essence of home spread like wildfire, enveloping entire neighbourhoods and reminding her how true wealth is, indeed, nothing more than the simple act of giving, nurturing, and loving.

Mia's reflections turned outward as she heard the laughter of children playing in the yard, their gleeful voices harmonizing with the spirit of the home they had built together. The budding friendships forged through shared experiences echoed the timeless belief that a rich home is not simply a place of residence but a beacon of light that guides the weary souls seeking solace. With the garden now blooming with the colours of joy, each blossoming flower reminded her that the seeds they planted together, rooted in community, had created a splendour that transcended the material world, crafting a space where everyone felt welcomed in the embrace of abundance.

The realization dawned upon Mia in moments of quiet reflection, that her life would be forever intertwined with this endless journey of love and community. This home, once discerningly beautiful yet empty, had now become a living witness to the stories of shared laughter, growth, and heartwarming friendships, enhancing the vibrant legacy in ways she had never believed possible. They stood together, hand in hand, laughing amid budding relationships, creating new memories destined to become cherished tales. Here, in this sanctuary, Mia felt the ebbs and flows of love, trust, and connection seeping into her very being, presenting her with the deep-seated understanding that family transcends blood ties, each moment shared with another composing a delicate love story in the tapestry of existence.

As the sun began to set on the horizon, casting radiant hues of orange and pink across the sky, Mia knew she had arrived home. Here, she was not merely housed; she was cradled in the arms of all that was good and enlightening in the universe. The warmth of the hearth glimmered brightly, illuminating paths that beckoned to her soul—for the quest for a rich home would continue, expanding beyond the walls she cherished into the world at large. She stood poised under the gathering dusk, heart open wide, ready to discover the infinite possibilities that awaited her with each breaking dawn. And in this journey, as she embraced the depths of love, the anchor of trust, and the unfathomable grace of community, Mia understood that her rich home would forever pulse with the warmth of shared hearts, manifesting beauty—a beauty that renewed itself and expanded into the boundless horizons of each day, becoming an endless journey of the soul.

ABOUT THE AUTHOR

Namdeo Bhagwandass is a first-time author whose life story is one of resilience, responsibility, and quiet strength. Raised in the face of profound hardship; losing his mother at a young age and growing up with an alcoholic father, he experienced instability and struggle early in life. Forced to mature quickly, he took on the responsibility of caring for his siblings while navigating life. These formative years shaped not only his character but also his purpose. Through adversity, he discovered an enduring belief in hope, and in the power of redefining what it truly means to have a 'rich' life.

Through his writing, Namdeo invites readers to reconsider what makes a home truly wealthy. His hope is that readers, especially those facing hardship, will find encouragement in his journey and begin to see that true richness is built from within.

Made in the USA
Monee, IL
12 November 2026

28e11a16-6e96-405a-a4f7-305f18a8d8e6R01